Equity and the Constitution

Gary L. McDowell

Equity
and the Constitution

The Supreme Court, Equitable Relief, and Public Policy

With a Foreword by
Henry J. Abraham

The University of Chicago Press
Chicago and London

GARY L. MCDOWELL is assistant professor
of political science at Dickinson College.

The University of Chicago Press, Chicago 60637
The University of Chicago Press, Ltd., London

Chapter 4 of this book was first published as
"Joseph Story's 'Science' of Equity" in the *1979
Supreme Court Review*, edited by Philip B. Kurland
and Gerhard Casper. Copyright © 1980 by The
University of Chicago. All rights reserved.

Library of Congress Cataloging in Publication Data

McDowell, Gary L., 1949–
Equity and the Constitution.

   Bibliography: p.
   Includes index.
   1. Equity—United States.   2. Political
questions and judicial power—United States.
3. United States. Supreme Court.   I. Title.
KD399.M32   347.73   81-16006
ISBN 0-226-55814-2   347.307

To Jerry, for always being there

Junius
*The Letters
of Junius,*
1769

If an honest, and I may truly affirm, a laborious zeal
for the public service, has given me any weight in your
esteem, let me exhort and conjure you never to suffer
an invasion of your political constitution, however
minute the instance may appear, to pass by, without
a determined, persevering resistance. One precedent
creates another—they soon accumulate and constitute
law. What yesterday was fact, today is doctrine. Examples are supposed to justify the most dangerous
measures; and where they do not suit exactly, the defect
is supplied by analogy. Be assured that the laws which
protect us in our civil rights, grow out of the constitution, and that they must fall or flourish with it.

Contents

Contents

Foreword

To endeavor to tackle the vexatious issue of equity is a brave and commendable aim in and of itself. To do so intelligently *and* intelligibly is as rare as it is laudable, and it is hardly astonishing that few have ventured forth into that dimly seen and imperfectly perceived corner of knowledge. We are hence fortunate indeed that Professor McDowell has been brave and enterprising enough to do so, and to do so without cant or nonsense: he calls a spade a spade, not a trowel. Moreover, he has succeeded admirably in elucidating, analyzing, and evaluating both the concept of equity and its application—in particular as a tool of the judicial process or, to put it more accurately, of the judicio-political process. At a time in our history when judges have become managers and administrators as part and parcel of their perceived judicial functions, running school boards, transportation services, hospitals, housing, state institutions for the insane, prisons; when, in effect, they have all but transformed the Constitution into an omnibus piece of legislation; when public policy is demonstrably, and evidently continuingly, made more by the judiciary than by the legislature, it is vital to take stock and ask whence this power derives and what tools it utilizes. When Thomas Paine remarked, "America has no monarch: Here the law is King," he referred to the law of the land. He would be surprised to find that, in our time, that law, at least in its public components, has been transformed into court-made, court-decreed law to a very considerable degree. As Professor

Foreword

McDowell's book demonstrates so incisively,
sophisticatedly, comprehensively, and literally—
even elegantly—the judicial tool that has been employed most effectively as a weapon in that transformation has been the equity power.

Equity, in common contemplation, begins where
the law ends; it supplies justice in circumstances not
covered by law; it is a system of jurisprudence that
augments or supplements the common law. It is *a
priori* a formidable weapon. Hence, as Mr. Chief
Justice Warren E. Burger confessed, or explained,
when he rendered the Court's unanimous opinion in
the seminal 1971 "forced busing" case of *Swann* v.
Charlotte-Mecklenburg Board of Education (402
U.S. 1)—that the Court here was invoking the
"judiciary's historic equitable remedial powers" by
upholding the utilization of "racial balances or racial quotas" in ordering the busing of students to
achieve desegregation—he pointed to that weapon
at once tellingly and candidly. That Section 2000c-6
of Title IV of the Civil Rights Act of 1964 seemed
quite specifically to forbid assignment on the basis
of racial quotas was brushed aside by the Justices
by applying the awesome power of equity "in the
quest for attaining full compliance with the spirit as
well as the letter of the equal protection of the laws
clause of the Fourteenth Amendment." In other
words, in resorting to its equity weapon, the Court
rejected the argument that the Civil Rights Act at
issue had demonstrably limited federal judicial authority when its Title IV had defined "desegregation" as "the assignment of students to public
schools and within such schools without regard to
their race, color, religion, or national origin . . . [and
that] 'desegregation' shall not mean the assignment
of students to public schools in order to overcome
racial imbalance."

The judicial use of the power of equity in the
Swann case is, of course, but one illustration—
albeit a celebrated one—of the potential enormity of
that power's range and extent, a syndrome which

Professor McDowell examines and discusses with such lucidity and insight. It is a source of considerable joy and pride to see one's student come to grips so honestly and so professionally with a phenomenon of such subtlety, yet of such centrality in the constitutional constellation that embraces government and politics in our land.

HENRY J. ABRAHAM
James Hart Professor of
Government and Foreign Affairs

University of Virginia
Charlottesville, April 1981

Preface

This study began as an attempt to uncover the constitutional source of the current period of judicial activism, which, unlike earlier periods of essentially proscriptive judicial assertiveness, has been decidedly prescriptive in its nature. The first question we tend to raise in response to such positive expressions of a judicial will as busing to achieve racial integration, educational enrichment programs to combat the lingering effects of segregation, and low-income-housing distribution in our cities is that of institutional capacity: Is the judiciary capable of making such policy choices? But there is a deeper question that we must ultimately raise, that of constitutional legitimacy: Is the judiciary, on the basis of the Constitution, legitimately empowered to make such policy choices?

The search for the constitutional source of a prescriptive judicial power led to the equity power granted by Article III of the Constitution. And this study, in turn, became more than a critical assessment of judicial activism; it became something of a history of American equity jurisprudence. What follows is an attempt to trace the transmission and transformation of the idea of juridical equity from its first appearance in Aristotle's writings through the recent opinions of the United States Supreme Court under Chief Justice Warren Burger.

In the course of completing an exercise such as this, one accumulates a great many debts. I was particularly fortunate to have access to several distinguished scholars who gave freely of their time, counsel, and criticism. I am most indebted, however, to my friends and teachers Henry J. Abraham and Robert A. Rutland, for whom I have not only the highest professional regard but also the deepest personal affection. Only rarely does one find such a high level of scholarship blended with such a deep dedication to teaching. They provided a constant flow of suggestions and encouragement and relentlessly strove to tame my vituperative prose. Where they succeeded, this study is so much the better.

I am very grateful to those who read and commented on various chapters as the study progressed and to those who tirelessly listened to my prosaic dilemmas and offered much good counsel: Robert Jennings Harris, Ralph A. Rossum, David K. Nichols, K. Robert Nilsson, Eugene W. Hickok, Jr., Jeffrey Poelvoorde, Tinsley Yarbrough, George Friedman, Jeffrey Sedgwick, and J. Mark Ruhl. Their patience and assistance, and, most of all, their friendship, are deeply appreciated.

Parham Williams, Joseph Bessette and Sotirios Barber read the entire manuscript with the kind of critical eye every author appreciates; their suggestions have made this a much better book than it would otherwise have been.

My colleagues and students in the Department of Political Science at Dickinson College have provided me with an atmosphere of collegiality, intellectual curiosity, and academic rigor that would be difficult to surpass. Victoria Kuhn—as always—was there to make sure that everything flowed smoothly; such diligence and kindness are rare. The entire project was generously supported by grants from the Dickinson College Faculty Committee on Research and Development.

My family generally, and my mother in particular, provided the continuous support and encouragement over the long haul without which nothing could have been accomplished. Of greatest importance, however, has been Karla. Her indefatigable reading, criticizing, typing, and retyping of the manuscript were surpassed only by her willingness to discuss equity for inequitably long periods of time. For her unfaltering moral support I owe much more than mere words can ever express.

Introduction

The Federal Farmer
October 10, 1787

It is a very dangerous thing to vest in the same judge power to decide on law, and also general powers in equity; for if the law restrain him, he is only to step into his shoes of equity, and give what judgment his reason or opinion may dictate.

From Equitable Relief to Public Policy

Until little more than two decades ago the federal judiciary held a position in the American political order quite removed from the policymaking function. Although the courts exercised immense political power in determining the constitutionality of legislative and executive actions, that power was essentially *proscriptive*. Since then, the judiciary has begun to exercise more than judgment in a good many instances, overflowing its former banks by offering *prescriptive* decrees in many areas of sensitive social policy. By doing so, it has opened itself to soundly reasoned criticism from nearly every quarter.[1]

With increasing frequency the federal judiciary has been assuming a new, positive, posture. From the opinions of Chief Justice Warren in *Brown* v. *Board of Education of Topeka, Kansas,** and Chief Justice Burger in *Swann* v. *Charlotte-Mecklenburg Board of Education,* to Judge Frank Johnson in *Wyatt* v. *Stickney,* Judge Virgil Pittman in *Bolden* v. *City of Mobile, Alabama,* and Judge Frank Battisti in *United States* v. *City of Parma,* the trend is clear: there is a willingness to enter into the "political thicket" and attempt to straighten out what the more representative institutions have allegedly failed to accomplish. The recent trend has been for the judiciary to move from a position of decreeing what the government cannot do to a position of decreeing what the government must do.

*Full citations are given in the List of Cases, preceding the Bibliography.

The most controversial prescriptive judicial decrees of the Supreme Court—*Brown* v. *Board of Education of Topeka, Kansas, Green* v. *County School Board of New Kent County, Alexander* v. *Holmes County Board of Education, Carter* v. *West Feliciana Parish School Board, Swann* v. *Charlotte-Mecklenburg County Board of Education, Keyes* v. *School District No. 1, Denver, Colorado, Lau* v. *Nichols, Milliken* v. *Bradley* (I and II), and *Hills* v. *Gautreaux*—all have rested ostensibly upon the same foundation: the equity power created by Article III of the Constitution. But they have rested on an understanding of that power that is new. Beginning with the two *Brown* v. *Board of Education* cases (1954 and 1955), the Court fused the idea of equity to the newly discovered right of psychological equal protection—a right of protection against a "feeling of inferiority"—to forge a new constitutional standard of equality *by* the law, rather than equality *before* the law. In particular, equity, which was originally understood as a judicial means of offering relief to individuals from "hard bargains"[2] in cases of fraud, accident, mistake, or trust, and as a means of confining the operation of "unjust and partial laws,"[3] has lately been stretched to offer relief to whole social classes. The original understanding of equity has been transformed into a "sociological" understanding that has undermined not only equity as a substantive body of law but the idea of equality as well.

In the process of this transformation of the idea of juridical equity, there has been a substantial loss of judicial appreciation for the great tradition of equity jurisprudence. The Court, in using its "historic equitable remedial powers" to impose its politics on society, is often forced to ignore or deny the great tradition of equitable principles and precedents, which had always been viewed as the inherent source of restraint in equitable dispensations.

I

In the Constitution, the equity power is not well defined; indeed, it is not defined at all. But the lack of constitutional definition in no way obscures what the Framers meant by "all cases in law and equity." For the Framers, as for us, the word was backed by several centuries of jurisprudence.

The substantive concept of juridical equity—from its first formulation by Aristotle, through the Roman tradition of Cicero and Justinian, through the efforts of such English and Scottish students of jurisprudence as Ranulph de Glanville, Henrici de Bracton, Christopher St. Germain, Sir Edward Coke, Sir Francis Bacon, Thomas Hobbes, Lord Kames, and Sir William Blackstone, and up to the Founders of the American republic—remained virtually unchanged. From one century to the next the idea was transmitted, with nearly every writer paying tribute to Aristotle's first pronouncement. In the *Rhetoric* Aristotle had pointed out:

> For that which is equitable seems to be just, and equity is justice that goes beyond the written law. These omissions [in the written law] are sometimes involuntary, sometimes voluntary, on the part of legislatures; involuntary when it may have escaped their notice, voluntary when, being unable to define for all cases, they are obliged to make a universal statement, which is not applicable to all, but only to most cases . . . ; for life would not be long enough to reckon all the possibilities. If then no exact definition is possible, but legislation is necessary, one must have recourse to general terms. [1374a][4]

Law, by its nature general, is limited and suffers the possibility of promoting injustice as well as justice in particular instances. It is necessary that there be a continuing opportunity for deliberation to reassert itself in the realm of positive law. Equity is the power to dispense with the harsh rigor of general laws in particular cases. But equity is always to be understood as the exception rather than the rule. Equity, from the beginning, was viewed as a part of the law, not as some power superior to it. Throughout the vast tradition of equity jurisprudence one maxim was held to be indispensable in the administration of equity: *Aequitas sequitur legem*—"Equity follows the law." Equity was necessary, in many cases, to fulfill the law. The law, being by its nature general in scope and application, always admits of exceptions. However, when the law did provide an adequate and complete remedy for alleged wrongs, an equity court was understood to have no authority to embellish or replace it. In particular, it was the common belief that a court of equity had no control over "imperfect obligations, resting upon conscience and moral duty only, unconnected with legal obligations."[5]

The major innovations in equity jurisprudence, following Aristotle, were in the procedural rather than the substantive realm. In Rome there first appeared a special office for the administration of equity. This idea was brought to its most complete institutional expression in England with the creation of the office of the chancellor, or "Keeper of the King's Conscience." Throughout the entire history of procedural innovations in equitable adjudication it was understood that equity is a potentially dangerous source of arbitrary discretion; and when kings came to be replaced by constitutions, the procedural arrangements for the dispensation of equity had to be reconsidered in light of this potential danger.

In America the debate was largely between those who followed the opinion of Sir Francis Bacon and those who followed that of Henry Home, Lord Kames. Bacon advocated a rigid separation between courts of law and courts of equity. Kames believed, to the contrary, that the separation of law from equity was a chimerical idea and that justice, if it were to be served, demanded that each court enjoy a mixed jurisdiction, reaching to both law and equity.

These older debates between Kames and Bacon over juridical equity were essentially different views on how to restrain this necessary but potentially dangerous power. One way differentiated equitable and legal pleadings, making clear that the former was a kind of last resort when the latter had been exhausted. The other way consolidated law and equity but in the process bound equity by rules and precedents through a law or "science" of equity, thus rendering it self-regulating.

But however glaring the differences over the procedural questions, Bacon and Kames were united on a deeper, substantive level. Beneath their differences was a crucial underlying agreement, that equity, though necessary to correct the harshness of strict law, could degenerate into arbitrary judicial discretion. Both believed that equity must be carefully restrained and hedged in order to curb its excesses without undermining its essential function.

The Founders chose to follow the tradition of Lord Kames. In the Philadelphia Convention they moved quickly and relatively quietly to vest in one supreme court, and such inferior courts as might be created, a judicial power that would extend to all cases in law and equity. The procedures for administering the power of equity—like the rest of the judicial power—the Convention chose to leave to Congress.

When the proposed Constitution emerged from the Convention, the fusion of law and equity was assailed by such keen-eyed Anti-Federalists as "Brutus" and the "Federal Farmer." To "Brutus," the provision for the judicial power would allow judges to "explain the constitution according to the reasoning spirit of it, without being confined to the words or letter," thereby granting them power "to mould the government into almost any shape they pleased."[6]

The "Federal Farmer" was equally wary of the proposed judiciary. In his view his countrymen were "more in the danger of sowing the seed of arbitrary government in this department than in any other." The lack of precision in defining the limits of equity in the Constitution was a serious defect that would contribute to "an arbitrary power of discretion in the judges, to decide as their conscience, their opinions, their caprice, or their politics" might demand. For if a judge should find that the "law restrain him, he is only to step into his shoes of equity, and give what judgment his reason or opinion may dictate."[7]

Whatever their reservations about the judicial power generally or the equity provision in particular, the Anti-Federalists were unable to thwart ratification of the Constitution. But, once it had been ratified, a good number of them took their places in the first Congress and there were able to influence to some degree the procedural arrangements of the new judiciary.

In the Judiciary Act of 1789, Congress effected something of a balance between those who advocated a hard separation of law from equity and those who argued for an unrestricted use of equity as a judicial tool in each federal court. While the act extended equity jurisdiction to all federal courts, it also established a firm rule as to when causes in equity could and could not be sustained. In the Process Act of 1792, Congress allowed that equity procedures in the federal courts would be "according to the principles, rules and usages which belong to a court of equity as contradistinguished from a court of common law." This act, as passed, gave the Supreme Court the discretion to make such regulations as it thought proper to prescribe equity procedure in the lower courts. In that year the Court, under Chief Justice John Jay, announced that in making such regulations it would "consider the practices of the Courts of Kings Bench and Chancery in England as affording outlines."[8]

The safety provided in the Judiciary Act of 1789 and the subsequent Process Acts was to separate rigidly the procedure of equity pleadings from the procedure of pleadings at law while leaving each court with the jurisdiction to entertain both. The draftsmen of these bills saw this procedural distinction as necessary if equity was to be kept from becoming a dangerous source of unfettered judicial discretion. This understanding was generally embraced by the judiciary as a fundamental maxim of American law.

In the nineteenth century, however, there began a movement to codify the common law in an attempt to reduce judicial discretion and render the administration of justice more efficient. A cardinal tenet of the Codification Movement was the merger of equity proceedings with legal proceedings. In time the Codifiers gained ground, and the merger of law and equity in the name of judicial efficiency and simplicity became commonplace. In 1938 the trend peaked in the Supreme Court of the United States with the adoption of the New Rules of Civil Procedure. In that body of rules the formal distinction between equity procedures and legal procedures was abolished.

By combining the procedures of law with procedures in equity, the Court in effect ignored the dangers of equity that had always lain at the core of its procedural arrangements. With the Rules of Civil Procedure of 1938, the Court made it convenient for judges to switch from their shoes of law to their shoes of equity whenever they found the law too restrictive, just as the "Federal Farmer" had warned. In its effort to reduce

7

equity to a safe and more certain code, the Court opened the door for the power of equity to be exercised with a disregard for precedent or procedure.

II

The underlying assumption of American constitutionalism is that there is an intimate connection between procedure and substance, and that the institutional arrangements of a polity have a direct bearing on its substantive actions. This understanding lay at the heart of the original separation of law and equity. By maintaining a procedurally distinct judicial system, equity would be kept from flowing over and giving the law an undue liberalism, and law would be kept from rendering equitable dispensations too rigidly bound. Each had its place in the American system; and to maintain its authority, each had to be kept in its place. The merging of equity procedures and legal procedures had one overwhelming effect. Without the rigid separation of pleadings, it was only a matter of time until equity no longer would be held as a necessary substantive body of law and would be viewed as merely another set of procedural remedies available to a court. Restraint through adherence to principle and precedent would be lost.

In *Porter* v. *Warner* (1946) the Court seemed on the verge of giving equity a radical expansion by arguing that when the "public interest is involved in a proceeding" the equitable powers of the federal district courts "assume an even broader and more flexible character than when only a private controversy is at stake." But it was not until 1955 that it became clear just how fluid equity had become. The Court, in the second *Brown* v. *Board of Education of Topeka, Kansas* case, fashioned a new understanding of the Court's equitable remedial powers. The central thrust was that in the place of an individual adverse litigant the Court placed an aggrieved social class. Its remedies would be decreed, no longer for the individual who had been injured by the generality of the law, but rather for whole classes of people on the basis of a deprivation of rights—a deprivation that was provable only by resort to the uncertain realm of psychological knowledge and sociological inference. Further, the Court went beyond decreeing discriminatory laws unconstitutional and restricting their operation: it attempted to fashion broad remedies for those so deprived.

What is particularly striking about Warren's invocation of the federal equity power in *Brown* (II) is that, while he spoke of the "traditional attributes" and guiding "principles" of equity being controlling, he then ignored most of the more substantial equitable principles in writing his decree. The effect was to present the lower federal courts with a virtual blank check.

The understanding of equity expressed in *Brown* (II) and its progeny differs from the traditional understanding in seven essential ways:

Old	New
Equitable and legal procedures separated.	Equitable and legal procedures merged.
Applied to specific individuals.	Applied to broad social groups.
Focused on specific concrete rights, especially property.	Focused on more abstract rights, especially equality.
Usually exercised in a *proscriptive* way to block the enforcement of an unjust law or action.	Greater emphasis on broad remedial mandates, hence generally exercised in a *prescriptive* way.
Largely bound by precedent.	Largely unbound by precedent.
Required an irreparable injury that was immediate, great, and clear.	Irreparable injury generally proved by a resort to social-science hypotheses.
Restricted by the federal principle.	Not restricted by the federal principle.

Since *Brown,* the Court has continued to expand, and to confuse the public perception of, its power of equity. The result has been to substitute social-science speculation for precedent and principle as the standard of both constitutional meaning and equitable relief. This new tradition of sociological equity has baffled even those of its defenders who have sought to define its scope. Chief Justice Burger was thus driven to conclude in *Swann* v. *Charlotte-Mecklenburg County Board of Education* (at 15–16) that "words are poor instruments to convey the sense of basic fairness inherent in equity. Substance, not semantics, must govern, and we have sought to suggest the nature and limitations without frustrating the appropriate scope of equity." The problem, of course, is that words are all we have. One must at least suspect that, if the limits of any governmental power cannot be clearly and forcefully articulated, then there is something desperately wrong with our understanding of that power.

III

The most prominent feature of this new concept of equity is the object addressed. Equity has now become the means of "reconciling public and private needs." What at the Founding was thought to offer relief to individuals from "hard bargains" has become a judicial power to draw the line between governmental powers and individual rights and to attempt to create remedies for past encroachments against whole classes of people. The Court in *Brown* (II) established the "equitable principles" doctrine to guide the judiciary in "fashioning and effectuating" their desegregation decrees, and that doctrine has survived through *Swann* v. *Charlotte-Mecklenburg* and is still alive and well in *Milliken* v. *Bradley* (II) and *United States* v. *City of Parma*. But this new equity power in no way need be limited to the desegregation cases. One need only recall Benjamin Cardozo's observation that it is the "tendency of a principle to expand itself to the limit of its logic"[9] to catch a glimpse of the possibilities.

The Court's fusion of equity to equal protection in the *Brown* cases has led to a distortion of its interpretations of the Constitution. It has led the Court to attempt to fashion broad equitable remedies for society from the particular cases or controversies brought before it. Equity, originally and historically a power addressed toward individuals, has been stretched to cover entire social classes. As a result, the individual adverse "litigant, though still necessary, has tended to fade a bit into the background."[10] And the Court has been steadily moving into the realm of legislation. Broad decrees "fashioned and effectuated" for the whole country on the basis of "equitable principles" are, in essence, judicially created social policies.

An older political science assumed that the formulation of policies that were to reach the lives of the people were more safely written by the duly elected representatives of the people. Through a rather intricate system of representation, it was believed that all the conflicting opinions, passions, and interests of the citizens could be filtered up into the legislature and, by a process of coalescing and politics, be fashioned into a public policy that resembled, at least somewhat, the public interest. It was never assumed that the judiciary was competent for that task. As Nathaniel Gorham pointed out to the delegates at the Philadelphia Convention, "Judges . . . are not to be presumed to possess any peculiar knowledge of the mere policy of public measures."[11] James Madison made the same point in *The Federalist,* No. 49, when he argued that the judiciary "by the mode of their appointment, as well as by the nature and permanency of it, are too far removed from the people to share much in their prepossession."[12]

The formulation of public policy is an expression of a political will. To be legitimate, such policies must reflect the will of the people, not the independent will of their deputies. The judiciary has no means available for ascertaining the public will in any meaningful sense. It is not, strictly speaking, a representative body. It must be assumed that the Court, when it moves to make decisions with respect to such matters as immediate integration of schools, busing, low-income-housing development, and remedial-education programs, is exercising not merely judgment: it is making policy choices; it is exercising its own will. It is exercising a power that the Constitution denies to it. The Court, under the guise of its "historic equitable remedial powers," has been endeavoring to formulate public policies for which it lacks not only the institutional capacity but, more important, the constitutional legitimacy.[13]

1

The Foundations of American Equity: Antecedents to 1792

Lord Kames   To determine every particular case, according to what is just, equal, and salutary, taking in all circumstances, is undoubtedly the idea of a court of equity in its perfection; and had we angels for judges, such would be their method of proceeding, without regarding any rules—but men are liable to prejudice and error, and for that reason cannot safely be trusted with unlimited powers. Hence the necessity of establishing rules to preserve uniformity of judgment in matters of equity as well as common law.

One The Jurisprudential Foundations of American Equity

The idea of equity that came to be drafted into Article III of the Constitution of the United States was not conceived in Philadelphia during the summer of 1787. As a juridical concept, equity's roots were firmly planted in the Western legal tradition; they went remarkably deep and straight, running through the English and Roman traditions all the way back to Aristotle. And it is to this Western tradition of equity jurisprudence that attention first must be paid in order to understand the foundations of American equity jurisprudence.

I

Aristotle was the first Greek writer to attempt to fashion a notion of juridical equity. Prior to Aristotle, *epieikeia* enjoyed various broad connotations: clemency, leniency, indulgence, or forgiveness.[1] But in all its different uses *epieikeia* stood in marked contrast to the law. It stood outside the sphere of strict law as a means by which the sharp edges of the law could be blunted. It was a great first achievement of Aristotle in the realm of jurisprudence to explain that *epieikeia* "constitutes only the corrective function of the law and is not something different from the law."[2]

Aristotle's ruminations on equity in a jurisprudential sense appear in three of his ethical works: the *Magna Moralia*, the *Nicomachean Ethics*, and the *Art of Rhetoric*. In that order, his idea is brought to fruition in the *Rhetoric* from the seed planted in the *Magna Moralia*.

15

In the *Magna Moralia,* Aristotle broached the subject this way:

> Now Equity, and the equitable . . . man, are distinguished by readiness to take less than their just legal right. Where the lawgiver is unable to make nice distinctions, but lays down broad general rules, a man who there stands aside, and is content with what the lawgiver would have assigned him had he been able to distinguish individual cases, is an equitable man. [1198b]

Aristotle's equitable man is not simply a self-sacrificer who willingly waives his just claims; rather, he waives only those legal claims that are insufficiently distinguished by the lawgiver. Thus equity points to the necessity of a particularly human faculty that enables a man to know how to distinguish between his essentially just claims and his broadly defined legal claims. This faculty Aristotle called "discrimination," which is "concerned with the same matters as Equity; namely those rights that the lawgiver has left insufficiently distinguished." Of these rights, Aristotle continued,

> The discriminating man has a keen appreciation. He recognizes that the lawgiver has passed them over, but that they are none the less rights. . . .
>
> Discrimination, then, is closely associated with Equity; the discriminating man discerns, and the equitable man acts according to that discernment. [1199a]

As one scholar has pointed out, the *Magna Moralia* "contains the whole Aristotelian concept of *epieikeia,* though still in a rather awkward formulation."[3] In particular, there is not at this point in his thought any clear distinction between the procedural and substantive aspects of equity.

In the *Nicomachean Ethics* Aristotle further refined his idea of equity and its proper relation to justice. "The source of the difficulty," he wrote,

> is that equity, though just, is not legal justice, but a rectification of legal justice. The reason for this is that law is always a general statement, yet there are cases which it is not possible to cover in a general statement. In matters therefore where, while it is necessary to speak in general terms, it is not possible to do so correctly, the law takes into consideration the majority of cases, although it is not unaware of the error this involves. And this does not make it a wrong law; for the error is not in the law nor in the lawgiver, but in the nature of the case: the material of conduct is essentially irregular. When therefore the law lays down a general rule, and thereafter a case arises which is an exception to the rule, it is then right, where the lawgiver's pronouncement because of its absoluteness is defective and

erroneous, to rectify the defect by deciding as the lawgiver would himself decide if he were present on the occasion and would have enacted if he had been cognizant of the case in question. Hence, while the equitable is just, and is superior to one sort of justice, it is not superior to absolute justice, but only to the error due to its absolute statement. [1137b]

Finally, in the *Art of Rhetoric*, Aristotle's thought came to full bloom. His reflections in the *Rhetoric* reveal that a clear distinction between the procedural aspects and the substantive aspects of equity has been reached. In speaking of the nature of law, he established that law is divided into the sphere of the written and the sphere of the unwritten and that the second sphere is further divided into moral and legal spheres. The moral sphere of the unwritten law embraces such things as gratitude to benefactors, rendering good for good, and helping one's friends, while the legal sphere of the unwritten law "contains what is omitted in the special written law." It is in this sphere that Aristotle located *epieikeia*:

For that which is equitable seems to be just, and equity is justice that goes beyond the written law. These omissions [in the written law] are sometimes involuntary, sometimes voluntary, on the part of the legislators; involuntary when it may have escaped their notice, voluntary when, being unable to define for all cases, they are obliged to make a universal statement, which is not applicable to all, but only to most cases; and whenever it is difficult to give a definition owing to the infinite number of cases, as, for instance, the size and kind of an iron instrument used in wounding; for life would not be long enough to reckon all the possibilities. If then no exact definition is possible, but legislation is necessary, one must have recourse to general terms. [1374a]

Such equity is necessary in that justice demands that "errors, wrong acts, and misfortunes must not be thought deserving of the same penalty" (1374b). This is the case because misfortunes are those actions neither intended nor vicious; errors are those actions intended but not vicious; while wrong acts are both intended and vicious.

For Aristotle, human weaknesses, as made manifest in errors and misfortunes, must be pardoned if equity and hence a higher justice than mere legal justice is to be achieved. It is necessary to look beyond the letter of the law in cases of error and misfortune to the spirit of the law; beyond the action itself to its moral purpose; and beyond what the man now appears to be, in the particular instance, to what he has always been generally. Such cases demand the leniency of arbitration rather than the strict observance of the law. Law by its very nature is limited and suffers the possibility of

17

promoting injustice as well as justice. The positive law, being conceived by men, suffers in kind: it is by its nature defective. In order to bring the positive law more closely into line with the demands of justice, it is necessary that there be a continuing opportunity for human reason to reassert itself in the realm of positive law. Both the rule of law and the rule of men are necessary components in man's attempt to achieve justice, but neither is sufficient. The rule of law lessens the possibility that discretion will be used arbitrarily and unjustly, while discretion lessens the severity of written law. Equity is a means of attempting to reconcile the demands of justice with man's ability to be just.

Although Aristotle thus recognized the necessity of equitable dispensation, he also saw the dangerous propensities of human discretion. Ultimately, for Aristotle, equity was something far less than a license for unfettered discretion. Equity, in the sense of dispensing with the harsh rigor of general laws in particular cases, is always to be understood as the exception rather than the rule. Properly enacted laws remain the primary means for a people to approximate justice. Aristotle's fear of judicial discretion merits repeating. It is proper, he wrote,

> that laws properly enacted, should themselves define the issue of all cases as far as possible, and leave as little as possible to the discretion of the judges; in the first place, because it is easier to find one or a few men of good sense, capable of framing laws and pronouncing judgments, than a large number; secondly, legislation is the result of long consideration, whereas judgments are delivered on the spur of the moment, so that it is difficult for the judges properly to decide questions of justice or expediency. But what is most important of all is that the judgment of the legislator does not apply to a particular case, but is universal and applied to the future, whereas the [judges] have to decide present and definite issues, and in their case, love, hate, or personal interest is often involved so that they are no longer capable of discerning the truth adequately, their judgment being obscured by their own pleasure or pain. [*Rhetoric* 1354a–b][4]

To an amazing degree the Aristotelian concept of juridical equity continues to be accepted. Generally, the only embellishment on his original observations has been in the procedural rather than the substantive realm. The basic innovations during the Roman and the English experiences were in the realm of institutional arrangements and a concern for developing a body of equity "law." As Sir Ernest Barker correctly remarked: "Greek 'equity' was based on an idea of fairness and humanity in some ways analogous to the idea underlying English Equity or the Roman *Ius Naturale;* but it was in no sense (as they were) a formulated body of law."[5]

II

The contribution of Rome to equity jurisprudence was as limited as its contribution to political philosophy generally. Basically, our debt to the Roman jurists extends only to their having preserved and transmitted the Greek contribution and to their first efforts at what can properly be called a rudimentary court of equity. The transmission of the Greek idea, however, did not occur without some modification; with Rome, equity, *aequitas,* came to be associated with the tradition of natural law.

Roman law embraced two elements: the *ius gentium* and the *ius civile.* *Ius gentium* was the law common to all nations, while *ius civile* was the law promulgated for Roman citizens. This dichotomy was seen as necessary, given the large population of aliens that was drawn to Rome. Gradually, through the influence of Stoic philosophy, *ius gentium* came to be associated with *ius naturale,* natural law, the law that is applicable to all nations *(gentes)* because it is law that reflects the common nature of mankind rather than citizenship. Once this association was made, Roman lawyers came to see the *ius gentium* as the "lost code of Nature," which was to be restored to Roman jurisprudence by the edict of the praetor. It came to be seen as part of the duty of the praetor to supersede the *ius civile* where necessary in order to restore the natural standard of justice in the Roman law. The point of contact between *ius gentium* and *ius naturale* was the notion of *aequitas* or, more precisely, *naturalis aequitas,* natural equity.

In his *Ancient Law,* Sir Henry Maine suggested that the source of Roman *aequitas* was commonly thought to have been the Greek word, *isotēs,* the idea of equal or proportionate distribution. Maine denied this interpretation, choosing instead as the germ of Roman equity the Latin *aequus,* which he found to carry more a sense of leveling than did *isotēs.*[6] But, as we have seen, the source of the Greek concept of equity was *epieikeia;* and etymologically this seems to be the likely source of Roman *aequitas.*[7] Whatever the linguistic evolution, the notion embraced in Rome reflected the same concern as Aristotle's: the means necessary to mitigate or buffer the rigor of the law. The real concern of Roman *aequus* or *aequitas* was not so much leveling as it was fairness or an equality of treatment.

Cicero in his *De Officiis* reached the same conclusion as had Aristotle. He wrote:

> A perversion of justice, some extremely clever but harmful interpretation of a statute, also is a frequent cause of wrongdoing. Hence we have the saying *Summum Ius Summa Iniuria,* "Extreme legality is the worse law," a proverb become a cliché by daily use. [1. 6. 19]

19

Elsewhere, in the *Ad Herennium,* he argued that:

> The constituent departments [of the law] are the following: Nature,
> Statute, Custom, previous Judgments, Equity, and Agreement. The
> Law rests on Equity when it seems to agree with truth and the general
> welfare.... [2. 13. 19–20]

For Cicero, justice was equity, "giving to each thing what it is entitled
to in proportion to its worth" (ibid., 3. 2. 3). And justice, for men it seems,
begins with law. In *De Legibus* Cicero has one of the interlocutors speak
to the nature of law and justice and hence of equity. "Law," the speaker
proclaims,

> is the highest reason, implanted in Nature, which commands what
> ought to be done and forbids the opposite. This reason, when firmly
> fixed and fully developed in the human mind, is Law. And so [the
> most learned men] believe that law is intelligence, whose natural
> function it is to command right conduct and forbid wrongdoing. They
> think that this quality has derived its name in Greek from the idea of
> granting to every man his own, and in our language I believe it has
> been named from the idea of choosing. For as they have attributed the
> idea of fairness to the word law, so we have given it that of selection,
> though both sides properly belong to Law. Now if this is correct, as I
> think it to be in general, then the origin of Justice is to be found in
> Law, for Law is a natural force; it is the mind and reason of the in-
> telligent man, the standard by which Justice and Injustice are mea-
> sured. [1. 6. 19]

Although the populace generally views law only as written decrees, true
law transcends mere written law to include what we may call right reason.
It is this right reason under the appellation of *aequitas* that may properly
intrude into the realm of the written law to make that law a more proxi-
mate rendering of the true demands of justice. The Romans recognized,
as had the Greeks before them, that there is quite naturally a discrepancy
between justice and law. The notions of *epieikeia* and *aequitas* allowed
public officials to trim general laws to fit particular cases.

The most innovative contribution of Rome to the tradition of equity lay
in its institutional arrangements for meting out equity. Unlike Greece,
Rome began to develop a body of equity "law" as the equitable dispensations were made by the praetor. The praetor administered the
"duties of the supreme judicial office." In order to avoid oppressive
official actions, the Roman people came to demand that any of their
magistrates "whose duties had any tendency to expand their sphere...
publish, on commencing his year of office, an edict or proclamation,
in which he declared the manner in which he intended to administer

his department." Each yearly edict of the new praetor was appended to those of his predecessor and came to be called the *edictum perpetuum*, or the continuous or unbroken edict. With the ascension of Salvius Julianus under the Emperor Hadrian, the yearly additions ceased. The Edict of Julianus "embraced therefore the whole body of equity jurisprudence, which it probably disposed in new and symmetrical order." From the time of the Edict of Julianus until the reign of Alexander Severus, equity jurisprudence was filled out by treatises on the edict written by a succession of "jurisconsults," parts of which have survived in the Pandects of Justinian. During this same period the praetor was the administrator of both law and equity, although the formal fusion of law and equity was not completed until the reforms of Justinian.[8]

The Roman tradition of equity jurisprudence, like Roman law generally, exerted a great influence on subsequent ages. Through the conquests made by its armies and later through the spread of the Church, Roman equity came to be preserved and diffused throughout the Western legal tradition, and the greatest repository of that tradition was Great Britain.

III

The influence of Rome on the English tradition of equity jurisprudence has been questioned and debated at some length.[9] However, the essence of the debate centers on the procedural rather than the substantive impact, and just how much the Roman praetor served as a model for the English chancellor is really a question of marginal significance. In substantive equity terms, i.e., equity understood as a concern for mitigating the law, the influence of Rome was as great as it was obvious.

Until the vestiges of Roman influence bubbled to the surface of English jurisprudence in the twelfth century, the idea of Roman equity, probably introduced into Britain much earlier, had lain dormant. For "neither equity as a system, nor equitable powers in the crown, were ever known to Anglo-Saxon England."[10] But when the influence surfaced in the earliest English tracts, it was in some instances quite clear that Roman thought on the nature of equity had been imported in its entirety.

The clearest example of the transmission of Roman thought into Britain is shown by the reliance of two very early writers, Glanville and Bracton, on the *Institutes* of Justinian. In the *Institutes*, Justinian offered a preface which read thus:

> The Imperial dignity should not only be supported by arms, but guarded by laws, that the people may be properly governed in time of peace as well as war; for a Roman emperor ought not only to be victorious in the hostile field, but should expel the iniquities of men

regardless of law; and become equally renowned for a religious observance of justice, as for warlike triumphs.[11]

Between 1187 and 1189, Ranulph de Glanville, who in 1180 had been made chief justiciary of all England, wrote what is considered to be the first English common-law treatise. In *De Legibus et Consuetudinibus Regni Angliae,* Glanville introduced his readers to the work with a clear imitation of Justinian's prefatory remarks:

> Not only must royal power be furnished with arms against rebels and nations which rise up against the king and the realm, but it is also fitting that it should be adorned with laws for the governance of subject and peaceful peoples; so that in time of both peace and war, our glorious king may so successfully perform his office, that crushing the pride of the unbridled and ungovernable with the right hand of strength and tempering justice for the humble and the meek with the rod of equity, he may both be always victorious in wars with his enemies, and also show himself continually impartial in dealing with his subjects.[12]

Writing some fifty years after Ranulph de Glanville, Henrici de Bracton, a judge of the King's Bench during the reign of Henry III, produced his *De Legibus et Consuetudinibus Angliae.* Bracton found Justinian's *Institutes* a valuable aid to his reflections, and began his treatise in the same spirit:

> These two things are necessary for a king who rules rightly, arms forsooth and laws, by which either time of war or of peace may be rightly governed, for each of them requires the aid of the other, in order that on the one hand the armed power may be in security, and on the other the laws themselves may be maintained by the use and protection of arms. For if arms should fail against enemies who are rebellious and unsubdued, the realm will so be without defence, but if laws should fail, justice will be thereupon exterminated, nor will there be anyone to render a rightful judgment.[13]

Both Glanville and Bracton incurred debts to Justinian's *Institutes* beyond their introductions.[14] Both understood equity to flow from discretion and not from blind adherence to the law, thus perpetuating the understanding of equity first formulated by Aristotle and absorbed by Rome.[15] In Bracton's *De Legibus* we find a sound distillation of equity jurisprudence up to his own time:

> Equity is the suitable adjustment of things, which in like causes seeks to administer like rights, and adjusts all things well on an equal platform, and it is termed equity, as being as it were equality, and it is

employed in things, that is, in the sayings and actions of men. Justice
reposes in the mind of the just; hence it is, if we would speak properly, we shall call a judgment equitable, not righteous, and a man
righteous, not equitable.[16]

Further, Bracton distinguished between justice—"a virtue"—and
jurisprudence—"a science"—and noted that, whereas justice is one of
the highest goods, jurisprudence is only an intermediate one, by which an
ascent is made toward justice. For jurisprudence is a knowledge of "divine and human things, the science of what is just and unjust." Noting
further that "natural right denotes an equitable right," Bracton concluded
that equity is that power to restore those who have erred; equity softens
the rigor of the law by appealing to natural right in contradistinction to
positive right.[17]

A matter that would prove to be of greatest significance for the
emerging notion of American equity jurisprudence in the eighteenth
and nineteenth centuries was the tendency in Justinian's *Institutes,*
Glanville's *De Legibus,* and Bracton's *De Legibus* to link equity with
property.[18]

Bracton's treatise was first published as a book in 1569, although it had
been written more than three centuries earlier, in 1244. Fifty years before
Bracton's *De Legibus* was published for wider distribution, another work
appeared that was to become a major force in the English tradition of
equity jurisprudence. In 1518 Christopher St. Germain's *Dialogues between a Doctor of Divinity and a Student in the Laws of England*[19] appeared and clearly and powerfully rearticulated the Aristotelian concept
of equity.

"Equity," St. Germain began, "is a right wiseness that considereth all
the particular circumstances of the deed, the which also is tempered with
the sweetness of mercy."[20] The problem, elucidated, again, by the *Dialogues,* is the imprecision that by nature exists in trying to fit positive
laws to natural law or justice. Law, we are again reminded, by its very
nature must be general; but justice demands that justice in particular
exceptions must not be sacrificed by too strict an adherence to the law. In
such exceptions to the general experience of men as may arise it is clear
that "to follow the words of the law were . . . both against justice and the
commonwealth. Wherefore in some cases it is necessary to [leave] the
words of the law, and to follow [what] reason and justice requireth, and to
that [extent] equity is ordained; that is to say, to temper and mitigate the
rigour of the law."[21]

St. Germain insisted that "equity followeth the law" insofar as it must
reflect the law's intent. Equity was not to be a means of subverting the law

but rather a means of bolstering the law, which is itself but the means to a higher end—justice. In following the intent rather than the words of the law, equity was to be a healthy complement to the law in its quest for justice.[22]

St. Germain's contribution to the tradition of equity jurisprudence was not only in transmitting the original Aristotelian concept to his British brethren but also in this treatment of it as having a practical application to English law. Sir Frederick Pollock's judgment that St. Germain displayed a "grasp and insight quite exceptional at the time" seems beyond dispute.[23]

With St. Germain's *Dialogues,* the transmission of substantive Aristotelian equity into English jurisprudence was secure. What was left was the question of where in the English system the equity power was to be lodged, and it was this debate that would color English equity through the time of the American Founding. The debate sprang from the growing fear on the part of the practitioners of the common law that equity would be put to political tasks. It came to be that the practitioners "of the common law regarded equity much as the lay people regarded all legal science, that is, as an inscrutable kind of magic, and rather black than white."[24]

IV

In considering the great tradition of English equity jurisprudence, it is essential that one keep in mind that, fundamentally, equity and the common law originated from the same procedure. They originated as "one undifferentiated system in the effort of the king to carry out his duty of furnishing security and justice to all in the community by making use of his prerogative power through his prerogative machinery."[25] If any chronological precedence must be given, it would have to be that the common law grew from equity rather than equity from the common law, equity being the more fundamental concern for natural justice in preference to strict legal justice. The history of equity in England reveals that it was not until the common law began to be considered a more rigid body of law, with the binding strength of precedent and its subsequent rules, that equity began to emerge as a distinct system. Once the common law lost its original flexibility, it was necessary that equity—still undefined and fluid—be available to bend the hard edges of the common law to fit particular exceptions.

It was not until the mid-fourteenth century that the first equity courts arose in England.[26] Their purpose was clear: to allow individuals who believed themselves without remedy or without adequate remedy before the common law to appeal to the king's conscience for a special dispensation. The monarch seems always to have referred these special petitions to his chancellor (usually an ecclesiastic), the Keeper of the Great Seal, for resolution. By the fifteenth century this practice had solidified into a Court of Chancery, and, by the end of the seventeenth century, "the Court of Chancery was not only a regular court of justice but had started on the road of technical and scientific elaboration."[27] By this process, the chancellor came to be viewed by many as second only to the monarch in the power he wielded.[28]

As this equity system was growing up, it was paralleled by the development of the common law and by the emerging notion that the common law, and hence the judiciary that administered it, enjoyed a position independent of the monarch and his prerogative. As this belief in the ultimate superiority of the rule of law to all other rule, including the monarchy itself, developed, it was inevitable that a conflict between the Court of Chancery and the other common-law courts—the King's Bench, Exchequer, and Common Pleas—would erupt.[29] When the eruption occurred, it found England's greatest jurist and student of the common law, Sir Edward Coke, pitted against England's greatest chancellor and student of equity, Sir Francis Bacon.

It is interesting to note that the same sources that had served to transmit the equity jurisprudence of Athens and Rome to England were the sources from which Sir Edward Coke drew his support for his claims of superiority for the common law: Glanville, Bracton, and St. Germain.[30] It is striking that both the claims of Coke in behalf of the higher-law status of the common law and the claims of the proponents of equity in the Court of Chancery relied on the idea of *ius naturale* for their support. Indeed, it may well be said that it was the concern for equity in the fifteenth and sixteenth centuries that kept alive the natural-law ideas to which Coke could turn for his authority in the seventeenth century.[31] Eventually these two claims, the one by the common law and the other by equity, to a status as "higher law" boiled down to the fundamental issue in the Coke-Bacon debate: whether or not the judgments of the common-law courts were reviewable in the Court of Chancery.

Edward Coke, before becoming a commentator on English law, had been a law reporter, crown attorney, chief justice of the Common Pleas, chief justice of the King's Bench, and member of Parliament. Before ascending to the bench, he had been "conspicuously subservient to the royal interest,"[32] but, once there, he took a strongly political stance, denying that the royal prerogative was ever to be considered above the law. Echoing Bracton's earlier claim, he proclaimed that "the king hath no prerogative, but that which the law and the land allows."[33] There was no question in Coke's judicial mind that the proper authority and interpreters of that law were not the king and his officials, such as the chancellor, but the judges.

As early as 1608, after sitting in Common Pleas only since 1606, Coke in

Fuller's Case insisted, much to the fury of the monarch, that "no King after the Conquest assumed to himself to give any judgment in any cause whatsoever, which concerned the administration of justice within this realm, but these were solely determined in the courts of justice." When the king objected to such presumptions, saying that he, too, had the power to reason as well as the judges, Coke responded at some length that, even though the king was endowed with "excellent science and great endowments of nature," he simply was not "learned in the laws of his realm of England" because such legal knowledge is not the result of natural reason but is the result of an "artificial reason and judgment," one that requires "long study and experience" before a man can truly grasp the fine nuances of the law.[34]

In 1615, only two years after the king had elevated Coke to the King's Bench, largely at Bacon's advice, in an attempt to lure him back into the royal fold, Coke began his assault on the right claimed by the Court of Chancery (at that time under Lord Chancellor Ellesmere) to interfere and overrule a common-law decision. In 1616 Coke was removed by the king, again at Bacon's urging, from the King's Bench simply because of his unwillingness to support the claims of the royal prerogative over the common law. Although he remained active in public life after his dismissal, Coke's greatest contribution to the English judicial tradition came in 1628, when the first volume of his *Institutes of the Laws of England* appeared. That first volume is a commentary on Littleton's *Tenures,* and it contains Coke's basic contribution to equity jurisprudence. In Section 21, he offers a definition of equity that is quite new. Not only is equity no longer based in any sense on the king's "conscience," but it derives from the essence of the "judicial" in contradistinction to the "executive" power. "Equities," Coke wrote:

> is a construction made by the judges, that cases out of the letter of a statute, yet being within the same mischiefe, or cause of the making of the same, shall be within the same remedie that the statute provideth: and the reason hereof is, that for the lawmakers could not possibly set down all cases in expresse terms....

He completed his thought by quoting, in Latin and at some length, his authority: Henrici de Bracton in his *De Legibus et Consuetudinibus Angliae.*[35] For Coke, the power of equity was inherently a judicial power; equitable dispensations, made to mitigate the severity of the received law, fall to the judges, not to the king. If the equity court, the Court of Chancery, should have the right to review common-law proceedings, then not only is equity wrenched from the judicial power but the law is reduced to a position of subservience to the royal whim. Like his fellow common-law practitioners, Coke saw this as an illegitimate manifestation of the monarchical authority.

Sir Francis Bacon stood opposed to Sir Edward Coke primarily on two grounds: first, equity jurisdiction ought to be separated from common-law jurisdiction; second, the equity jurisdiction of the great Court of Chancery must be considered the supreme judicial tribunal—"the Court of [the King's] absolute power"—able to review the judgments made by the common-law courts. What Bacon focused his powerful attention on was Coke's claim of autonomy for the common-law courts from Chancery and his claim for a judiciary independent of the sovereign and empowered under the rule of law.

Bacon was always concerned with maintaining the certainty of the law. To this end he saw as essential the careful control of judicial discretion. This was the basis of his conclusion that courts of law and of equity should be maintained separately. If not, judges could, under claims of equity, mutilate the law, serving not to supplement but to supplant it. Should law and equity come to be fused, the law would certainly be devoured by equity; the certainty of properly enacted and promulgated laws would be sacrificed to the arbitrary discretion of a single man's reasoning.[36] In sum, "Bacon sought to reduce the pretension of the common-lawyers to make law by interpretation, popular men popularly legislating free from the check of Chancery."[37] The danger Bacon saw in the fusion of law with equity was that judges would cease to judge and begin to legislate.

There was no systematic treatise on equity left by Sir Francis Bacon, but fortunately we have what is perhaps the next best thing. In 1681 Thomas Hobbes wrote *A Dialogue between a Philosopher and a Student of the Common Laws of England,* in which he took up Bacon's basic position and attacked the notions of Sir Edward Coke. Broadly speaking, Hobbes's *Dialogue* deals with the relationship of law to reason; more specifically, it deals with the old Bacon-Coke dispute over the relationship of equity and Chancery to the common law.

Hobbes's *Dialogue* is a significant contribution to the tradition of equity jurisprudence in that equity is now joined to a new concept of natural law, one far removed from the Ciceronian and Christian traditions. The *Dialogue* is in many ways an elaboration of the ruminations that Hobbes first presented in *Leviathan.* In that more celebrated work, he had presented equity unqualifiedly as his eleventh law of nature:

> Also if a man be trusted to judge between man and man, it is a precept of the Law of Nature, that he deale Equally between them. For without that, the controversies of men cannot be determined but by warre. . . .

27

The observance of his law, from the equall distribution to each man of that which in reason belongeth to him, is called EQUITY and (as I have sayd before) distributive justice.[38]

Later, in the second book of *Leviathan,* Hobbes went even further and designated equity as "that principall Law of Nature."[39] But one must not forget Hobbes's new understanding of the law of nature. In *Leviathan* he had earlier confessed that the "Lawes of Nature, which consist in Equity, Justice, Gratitude, and other morall vertues" are prior to the establishment of civil society, "not properly Lawes, but qualities that dispose men to peace and to obedience." These qualities become laws only after the commonwealth is settled "and not before; as being the commands of the commonwealth; and therefore also Civil Lawes: For it is the Sovereign Power that obliges men to obey them." To make such "morall vertues" as equity binding requires the awesome strength of sovereignty, the mighty Leviathan. And the sovereign power is itself the source of the judicial power. Hobbes found the notion of an independent judiciary as absurd as had Bacon before him. He begins his attack against the infidel Coke here in *Leviathan,* firing his warning shot, the echo of which carries through the *Dialogue.* His observation merits repeating:

That Law can never be against Reason, our Lawyers are agreed; and that not the Letter (that is, every construction of it) but that which is according to the intention of the Legislator, is the Law. And it is true: but the doubt is, of whose Reason it is, that shall be received for Law. It is not meant of any private Reason; for then there would be as much contradiction in the Lawes as there is in the Schooles; nor yet, (as Sir Edward Coke makes it) an *Artificial perfection of Reason, gotten by long study, observation and experience,* (as his was). For it is possible long study may encrease and confirm erroneous Sentences: and where men build on false grounds the more they build, the greater is the ruine: and of those that study and observe without equal time, and diligence, the reasons and resolutions are, and must remain discordant: and therefore it is not that *Juris Prudentia,* or wisedome of subordinate Judges, but the Reason of this our Artificial Man the Commonwealth, and his Command, that maketh Law: And the Commonwealth being in their Representative but one person, there cannot easily arise any contradiction in the Lawes; and when there doth, the same Reason is able by interpretation, or alteration, to take it away.[40]

In his polemical attack on Coke in the *Dialogue,* Hobbes conceded that equity is "a certain perfect reason that interpreteth and amendeth the law written," but he was then baffled how such a concept could be kept from frustrating "all the laws in the world."[41] However, he then made clear the solution: equity courts must be separate from the courts of law in order to allow a remedy to the defective judgments of the common-lawyers.[42] Equity, being properly understood to be "right reason," is, in essence, natural reason. Therefore, it is accessible to kings and even bishops as well as to judges. It is not, as Sir Edward Coke maintained, accessible only to those who labor in the minutiae of the law and who have developed their "artificial reason"; indeed, it is precisely this artificial reason of the lawyers that causes the necessity of separate courts of equity. The "Written Law" cannot, for Hobbes, be against "Reason"; but then the written law is not "signified by grammatical construction of the Letter [of the law], but that, which the legislator thereby intended should be in Force."[43] And it is in determining this spirit underlying the letter of the law that judges are apt to go astray: "for there is scarce any thing so clearly written, that when Cause thereof is forgotten, may not be wrested by an ignorant Grammarian or a Cavilling Logician, to the Injury, Oppression, or perhaps Destruction of an honest Man."[44] There must therefore be a source to whom the aggrieved party may appeal, and the appropriate source is the Court of Chancery, the conscience of the king.

This great debate between Edward Coke on the one side and Francis Bacon and Thomas Hobbes on the other seems never to have been settled. Indeed, the issue was still very much alive and raging at the time of the American Founding.

Nearly a century later, on the eve of the Revolution, the Scots were still mulling over the question of separating equity jurisdiction from legal jurisdiction. As was the case during the Coke-Bacon-Hobbes debate, the substantive nature of equity was securely established for the Scots, and there remained a fundamental reference to property in almost all cases in equity. In 1766, Henry Home, Lord Kames, produced his *Principles of Equity*,[45] coming down on the side of Sir Edward Coke in advocating the unity of law and equity in all courts of justice and against Bacon and Hobbes and the separation. Interestingly, the debate for the Founders came to be couched in terms of Bacon versus Kames rather than Bacon versus Coke.

For Lord Kames, equity remained the best means of correcting the "imperfections in the common law" by supplying "a defect in words, where will is evidently more extensive" and by rejecting words that "unwarily go beyond will."[46] Courts of equity are "impelled by the principle of justice...to correct or mitigate the rigour, and...injustice of the common law." To some extent, however, Kames's equity jurisprudence did hedge toward an embellishment of the substantive meaning of equity by introducing into the discussion the peculiar contribution of the Scottish Enlightenment's political philosophers, the moral-sense theory of human nature. But in much the same way that Hobbes's equity jurisprudence had suggested substantive additions, Kames's concern with benevolence (like Hobbes's association of justice with fulfilling covenants) points more to a change in the understanding of where the equitable disposition of man is lodged rather than in any alteration in the meaning of the word strictly construed. The word "equity" for Hobbes and Kames carried much the same connotation as *epieikeia* had for Aristotle and *aequitas* had for Cicero: a sense of fairness, leniency, or equality of treatment before the law. What had changed from antiquity to modernity was not the meaning of "equity" but rather the meaning of "justice." Equity still had its primary reference to law, which was still the means of attempting to achieve justice; but justice was now something lower than it had been for the ancients.[47]

Perhaps Kames's greatest single contribution to the tradition of Anglo-American equity jurisprudence was his concern for establishing a "system" of equity. He was clear in his reasoning:

> To determine every particular case, according to what is just, equal, and salutary, taking in all circumstances, is undoubtedly the idea of a court of equity in its perfection; and had we angels for judges, such would be their method of proceeding, without regarding any rules—but men are liable to prejudice and error, and for that reason cannot safely be trusted with unlimited powers. Hence the necessity of establishing rules to preserve uniformity of judgment in matters of equity as well as common law.[48]

Having come down more or less on the side of Coke in arguing for the union of law and equity in the courts of common law, Kames still recognized the problem of unbridled judicial discretion in much the same sense that Hobbes had recognized it. However, Kames's solution was not the ultimate and absolute authority of Leviathan; his solution was more modest and perhaps even more devastating. Kames sought the binding power of precedent to chain the judges down. Indeed, he went so far as to conclude that, since there "cannot be any other check upon a court of equity but general rules," no judge ought to "interpose unless he can found his decree upon some rule that is equally applicable to all cases of the kind."[49]

In one sense Lord Kames must be credited with being the father of modern equity jurisprudence. By advocating control of equity courts by strict adherence to precedent he was not really suggesting something boldly new but was only articulating and advocating the expansion of the natural tendency of equity decrees. It is the tendency of such judgments that, once decreed, they tend to become the standard for all similar cases in the future. What was originally a departure from the common law becomes a rule in equity. Thus it seems that equity contains within itself the self-regulating mechanism Kames advocates. But Kames appears to have been the first to see the inherent contradiction in the logic of equitable dispensations as a means of fettering judicial discretion. In this way, Kames paved the way for the nineteenth-century students of a science of equity whose demands for the "rationalization" of civil procedure would contribute greatly to what one scholar has called the rise of formalism and the "final and complete emasculation of Equity as an independent source of legal standards."[50]

One of the later writers into whose hands Kames's *Principles of Equity* fell was the author of the *Commentaries on the Laws of England,* Sir William Blackstone.[51] This student and teacher of the common law in a sense completed what Kames only began, and he did so by denying the validity of the distinction between courts of equity and courts of law. Blackstone argued that

> Equity . . . in its true and genuine meaning, is the soul and spirit of all law: *positive* law is construed and *rational* law is made by it. In this, equity is synonymous to justice; in that, to the true sense and sound interpretation of the rule. But the very terms of a court of *equity,* and a court of *law,* as contrasted to each other are apt to confound and mislead us: as if one judged without equity, and the other was not bound by law.[52]

Equity courts had derived originally from "imperial and pontifical formularies, introduced by their clerical chancellors," while courts of law had emerged from the feudal customs that prevailed in the ages of the Saxon and Norman judicatures; but, whatever their differences in origin, both now had come to rest, in Blackstone's view, on the same basis: "equally artificial systems, founded in the same principles of justice and positive law."[53] The only essential difference remaining was the "different modes of administering justice in each; in the mode of proof; the mode of trial; and the mode of relief."[54] Perhaps the greatest similarity that emerged was the fact that courts of equity and courts of law were both hemmed in by "effectual rules," which severely restricted the arbitrary discretion of the judges and secured certainty in the administration of justice. Blackstone firmly admonished any doubters by suggesting that

> if a court of equity were still at sea, and floated upon the occasional opinion which the judge who happened to preside might entertain of conscience in every particular case, the inconvenience that would arise from this uncertainty, would be a worse evil than any hardship that could follow from rules too strict and inflexible.[55]

The great men who since Lambard had held the great seal in Chancery and administered equitable relief had, already by Blackstone's day, "erected a system . . . of equity into a regular science which [could not] be attained without study and experience any more than the science of law."[56] And this great body of precedential equity rules had gone quite far in containing arbitrary opinion and guarding against any judicial "exercise of dictatorial power," which might ride over the law of the land, attempting to correct, amend, and control it by the "loose and fluctuating dictates of the conscience of a single judge."[57]

V

On the other side of the Atlantic, the great Western tradition of equity jurisprudence, from Aristotle to Blackstone, was readily available to those attempting to establish a republican form of government among thirteen loosely united states. In 1755 John Taylor's *Elements of the Civil Law*[58] had provided a convenient survey of equity jurisprudence from Aristotle on up. Taylor had carefully transcribed the ancient authorities and had attempted to sort through the tradition in a systematic way. Earlier, in 1737, Henry Ballow's *A Treatise of Equity*[59] had appeared, and, like Taylor's *Elements,* it served as a handy source book. The problem posed by equity jurisdiction and chancery courts was not settled for the Americans; it was still very much before the public eye. In a way, the problem was painful, for chancery courts represented to the Americans part of the political corruption that was England. To a people dedicated to the rule of law, the proper relationship of law to equity was a difficult question but one that would soon have to be addressed and answered.

Two The Constitution and the American Idea of Equity

The English legal tradition in the realm of equity jurisprudence, as in so many other aspects of the law, came to exert an influence in the colonies that was at once positive and negative. The great tradition of the common law was perhaps the most effective teacher of law available to the Americans, but the institutional arrangements that had evolved in England for the administration of that law came increasingly to be viewed as founts of corruption and the primary source of the colonists' troubles. Looking to the seventeenth-century polemics on the nature and causes of free government, the colonists began to fashion their own conception of the law, and it embraced above all else the idea that a written constitution is essential to free government. Whereas under the English constitution, constitutional questions were legal questions, the Americans began to draw a rigid distinction between what were properly constitutional questions and what were properly legal questions. Ultimately, this distinction between constitutional and legal matters manifested itself in the notion of the higher-law foundation of American constitutionalism.[1] But despite the highminded rhetoric of the higher-law proponents, a basic administrative problem remained: how to bring the "higher" law to bear on the "lower" law without losing the efficacy and virtue of the higher law in the hands of mere men, disposed as they naturally are to error and prejudice in their interpretations.

I

If the American legal system of the colonial period were to be described in one word, that word would surely be "confusion." By their provincial status, the thirteen colonies were naturally under the legal jurisdiction of England. But English law was best suited for England, and it often failed to meet the exigencies of the new rough-and-tumble land of America. As a result, American colonial law came to resemble more a patchwork quilt than a finely woven fabric. The common law was sewn together with statute law, custom, and the strong colonial spirit of innovation in order to meet the problems of the new and restless society. To deal with this legal patchwork called for great resourcefulness on the part of judges; the result was an enormous amount of judicial discretion. "The consequence for colonial jurisprudence was both flexibility and uncertainty."[2] This uncertainty caused a growing distrust of the judiciary. One disgruntled colonist complained that unbridled judicial discretion meant that "the issues of a cause depended not so much on the right of a Client, as on the breath of the Judge."[3] Part of this confusion was attributable to blurred jurisdictions among the different courts and, for the most part, an absence of a distinct equity jurisdiction, which in England had usually been administered in the Court of Chancery.[4] Instead of distinct equity courts, nearly all common-law jurists took it upon themselves to administer equity, and it appears that both law and equity were quite often sacrificed to arbitrary judicial opinion. In reflecting on the condition of the judicial power in Pennsylvania, John Dickinson grumbled as early as 1756 that almost

> every court there is a court of equity, for both judges and juries think it hard to deny a man that relief which he can obtain nowhere else, and without reflecting that equity never intermeddles but where the law denies *all manner* of assistance, every judgment, every verdict is a confused mixture of private passions and popular error, and every court assumes the power of legislation.[5]

The growing American enthusiasm for the notion of a "higher-law" constitution further added to this confused state of legal procedure. On the one hand, the idea of a higher law was rooted in the appreciation of the tradition of natural law and demanded that all law conform to the dictates of reason and natural equity.[6] On the other hand, it required that mere arbitrary discretion, based as it was on the inherently fallible reasoning of men, should not be permitted to supersede the law. The question that needed to be answered was whether an emphasis on the reason and equity of the higher law could be realized in their positive law in the absence of broad judicial discretion. Then, as now, the answer was in no way clear.

But it seemed to a growing number of concerned colonists that an attempt
to codify and systematize the common law was necessary in order to hem
in the increasingly troublesome prerogative of the judges. This practice—
codification—received theoretical support from the Beccarian observation, then regaining currency that, "in republics, the very nature of the
constitution requires the judges to follow the letter of the law."[7] It was
thought that, in order to return the rambunctious judges to republican
control, they would have to be reduced to "mere machine[s],"[8] and the
republican reduction of the judiciary was best to be achieved through the
antecedent jurisprudential reduction of the common law and reason and
equity to strictly enumerated statutes. But it was soon discovered that
strict codification was not the solution.

An attempt to state the law clearly and precisely would mean a massive
accumulation of statutory law. Such a stack of legal parchments would in
turn demand the cultivation of the "artificial reasoning" of lawyers to
decipher it and would not be readily accessible to the "natural reasoning"
of the self-governing populace. But, as Jefferson had observed, "The
great principles of right and wrong are legible to every reader: to peruse
them requires not the aid of many counsellors."[9] It appeared that in the
end this growth of statutory law would prove not only unhealthy but
futile; for ultimately no number of legal statutes could satisfactorily provide for the resolution of all questions of law. There would always be the
peculiar exception to the general rule upon which the statute had been
based and thus the necessity of human reason to trim the general rule to fit
the particular circumstance so that justice might be served.

By the mid-1780s the Americans were beginning to swing back toward
an understanding of law and politics that recognized the necessity of both
the rule of law and the rule of men and, in their disappointment, to swing
away from their evangelical faith in legislative supremacy. During this
swing from popular faith to popular skepticism of the legislative counsels,
the judiciary began to ascend in the estimation of the people.

II

Part of the original distrust of the judiciary stemmed from its close association, in the minds of the colonists, with the executive magistracy. Indeed, it was not until the notion of an independent and coordinate judicial
branch began to gain currency that public opinion would begin to consider
the courts a safe depository of the republican concern for reason and
equity in the law. During the 1780s, as the doctrine of separation of
powers began to be bolstered by the experiences of the states with tyran-
nical legislatures, both the executive and the judiciary began to be viewed

35

in a more favorable light. Legislative tyranny had been felt, and the only apparent guard against future encroachments had to rest in the coordinate branches of government power—the executive and the judiciary.

During the postrevolutionary heyday of legislative supremacy, juridical equity—that power to trim the edges of the written law to fit particular cases when a strict adherence to the written law would produce undue hardship—had been rendered impotent by the greater faith that legislative enactments themselves were more just than juridical discretion. By the mid-1780s, however, it began to appear that, in order to maintain the connection between the positive law and the higher law, it would be necessary to reinvest the judiciary with the power of equity. One American explained that this was necessary in order to restrain the "imaginary omnipotence" of legislatures "within the bounds of *reason, justice, and natural equity*."[10] Gradually, state courts began to reassert their authority to "determine causes according to equity, as well as positive law," so that they might serve "to prevent a failure of justice." And, since this judicial assertion was accepted by the public in practice, there came a resurrection of the theoretical understanding of the relationship between law and equity that had been embraced by Sir Edward Coke and Lord Kames: "there cannot be anything more absurd than a distinction between *law* and *equity*."[11]

When the political exigencies of the time drove the members of the Confederation to assemble in Philadelphia in 1787, they took with them not only their own experiences with equity jurisdiction but also a theoretical defense of why the judicial power must extend to both law and equity. Thus, when the time came, the Founders quietly moved to fuse law and equity in the separate and coordinate judicial power created by the Constitution.

III

Late in the Philadelphia Convention of 1787 the motion to extend the judicial power to both law and equity was passed with only a single objection. There was no debate at that time, and the issue never again arose.[12] But even though the usually rich records of the Convention are in this instance barren, other sources enable us to understand the logic underlying this nearly unanimous decision to fuse law and equity in Article III of the Constitution. The most important single source is, of course, *The Federalist,* which contains Alexander Hamilton's clear defense of the action.

There is little wonder why Hamilton assumed the task of explaining and defending the judicial provisions of the new Constitution to his fellow New Yorkers. He was, after all, one of that state's preeminent lawyers, and he carried to the ratification struggle a persuasive familiarity with all aspects of the law, including equity, that his partner James Madison lacked. Indeed, as the biographer of Hamilton's legal career has pointed out, "anyone practicing law in Hamilton's time must have found it necessary to be well versed in equity jurisprudence."[13] This was due to the fact that most of the litigation in New York's Court of Chancery was of a decidedly commercial flavor; most of the suits involved accounting, bonds, contracts, frauds, insurance, and bills of exchange.[14] During every year between 1784 and 1804, attorney Hamilton had cases pending in the Court of Chancery.[15]

Of all the cases he handled during the Confederation period, one stands out as the first example of Hamilton's jurisprudence that would later blossom in *The Federalist*. In *Rutgers* v. *Waddington* (1784) we see a clear exposition of the notion of judicial review that Hamilton would come to defend in the elegant prose of the seventy-eighth paper of *The Federalist*. But *Rutgers* is of interest to this study because it also presents Hamilton's early reflections on the nature of equity and its relationship to the law.[16]

The case of *Elizabeth Rutgers* v. *Joshua Waddington* arose under one of the anti-Loyalist acts of the New York Legislature, the Trespass Act of 1783. Mrs. Rutgers' property, a brewery and a malthouse, had been seized by the British commissary general for the use of English troops after Mrs. Rutgers had fled New York City when it was taken by the British in 1776. Two years later, the commissary general, Daniel Weir, signed the property over to two English merchants, Benjamin Waddington and Evelyn Pierrepont, through their agent, Joshua Waddington. They occupied the property rent free until 1780, when the British finally demanded that rent be paid. Between 1780 and 1783 Waddington and Pierrepont regularly paid their rent and made vast improvements on the property, which had been "stripped of everything of any value" before it was signed over to them. In the summer of 1783 the occupants were ordered to transfer their rent payments to the owner's agent, Anthony Rutgers. After what appear to have been several good-faith efforts by Waddington and Pierrepont to negotiate with Anthony Rutgers, who "constantly declined" to say what rent he demanded, they ultimately offered to turn over the property, complete with the additions and improvements they had made. Rutgers finally became inclined to discuss the matter, but he asked not only what the renters had offered but a staggering £1,200 in back rent. Shortly after the British evacuated the city, the brewery was reduced to ashes by a fire, which caused a loss to Waddington and Pierrepont of "upwards of £4,000." When approached again by the merchants to settle the dispute, Rutgers remained disagreeable. In February,

1784, a suit for £8,000 was brought for the rent in the Mayor's Court of the City of New York by Elizabeth Rutgers against Joshua Waddington, the British merchants' agent. The case became a symbol of the Whig-Tory, patriot-loyalist animosities still burning brightly. The heat of the controversy increased considerably when Alexander Hamilton, the so-called "Tory champion," joined the defense.

Elizabeth Rutgers brought suit under the Trespass Act to recover damages for the occupation of her property. Had the Trespass Act not existed, she would have had recourse for remedy in common-law trespass *quare clausum fregit* ("he broke the close"—breaking the close being an unlawful entry upon land). This common-law principle had developed from the principle that an individual's rights in his real property must be protected. Trespass *quare clausum fregit* allowed for justifiable trespass in pursuit of the "public good," but Waddington's intrusion could not be so claimed. Waddington's defense therefore had to appeal to the law of nations, which held that such occupation of abandoned real estate as had taken place was justifiable in wartime under the orders of the military command. The Trespass Act prohibited the pleading of military justification and thus presented itself in direct conflict with the law of nations.

Early in the proceedings Waddington's counsel prepared to seek removal of the case to the New York Court of Chancery and recourse to equitable rather than legal principles; however, the removal was never initiated. Hamilton saw a larger question in this test case. He came to see it as a conflict presented by a statute (in this case, the Trespass Act, which endeavored to block Waddington's common-law defense by an action of trespass *quare clausum fregit*) that violated not only the accepted law of New York (the common law) but also the treaty of peace that had been made by the United States. Had the case been removed, this larger question would undoubtedly have gone unanswered. But in choosing to pursue what he saw as the more fundamental question, the relation between statutory law and higher law, Hamilton was able effectively to retain the concern for equity within the broader framework. And in the case of Elizabeth Rutgers, the Cokean concept of the inherent unity of law and equity found judicial acceptance.

The initial effort to have the case removed to Chancery was outlined in the first brief of the defense team. This brief is significant in the history of American equity jurisprudence for the authority it invokes: Lord Kames's *Principles of Equity*. The issue was clear. Waddington, a *bona fide* tenant, had in good faith regularly paid the rents required of him to a "*Bona fide* possessor," the English, and therefore ought to be excused from the damages claimed against him by the true owner of the property, Elizabeth Rutgers. Even though by law Rutgers' claim was valid, such "Causes of

an Extraordinary nature'' as this, which required ''some singular remedy,'' were best suited as a subject ''of Decision for a Court of Equity.''
This was true, the brief had begun, because ''A Court of Common Law
considers only whether the Action be founded in Law—a Court of Equity
adds another Consideration, whether it be just and fair in the Plaintiff to
insist on the Action.''[17]

Although this narrower question remained, Hamilton was able to reach
the broader question by drawing out that the common law was in-
extricably linked to considerations of equity. In the sixth brief of the
defense, Hamilton made his move. His argument proceeded thus:

> The best way to construe statutes is by the rules of common law.
> When the provisions of a statute are general, they are subject to the
> control of the *common law* and may be construed contrary to the gen-
> eral words to render them agreeable to Natural Justice.
> Many things within the letter of a statute are not within its Equity
> and Vice-versa.
> No statute shall be construed so as to be inconvenient or against
> reason.
> Laws giving remedy where there was none before are to be con-
> strued strictly. When Statutes contradict the essential policy and
> maxims of the common law, the common law shall be preferred.

Hamilton follows up this line of logic with numerous ''Examples of construing statutes by Equity.'' His point is clear: equity demands that account be taken of the spirit as well as the letter of the law because ''In
Law as in Religion THE LETTER KILLS THE SPIRIT MAKES ALIVE.''[18]
Therefore, the attempt to separate law from equity is fundamentally
flawed, and the equitable questions of *Rutgers* v. *Waddington* are easily
answered by recourse to the common law, which is the accepted fundamental law of the state, superior to mere legislative enactment. The idea
of a judicial power split between law and equity is untenable. Questions of
law are interwoven with questions of equity, and questions of equity have
the law as their primary point of reference.

The opinion of the court, written by Mayor and Chief Judge James
Duane, reveals that Hamilton's logic was compelling. Duane explained
that the

> supremacy of the legislature need not be called into question; if they
> think fit *positively* to enact a law, there is no power which can control
> them. When the main object of such a law is clearly expressed, and
> the intention is manifest, the judges are not at liberty, altho' it appears
> to them to be *unreasonable* to reject it: for this were to set the *judicial*
> above the legislative, which would be subversive of all government.
> But when a law is expressed in *general* words, and come *collateral*

39

matter, which happens to arise from those general words is *unreasonable*, there the Judges are in decency to conclude, that the consequences were not foreseen by the Legislature; and therefore they are at liberty to expound the statute by equity, and only *quod hoc* to disregard it.

When the judicial make these distinctions, they do not control the Legislature; they endeavor to give their *intention* its proper effect.

The court then concluded that the consequence of the Trespass Act on Waddington "was not foreseen by the Legislature," and hence the court thus had the obligation "to explain it by equity, and to disregard it in that point *only*, where it would operate . . . unseasonably."[19]

In *The Federalist*, Hamilton was able to develop further the line of reasoning on the relation of equity to law that he had sketched in his arguments in *Rutgers*. In *Federalist*, No. 78, the first of five papers dealing with the judiciary, Hamilton assured his readers that the judicial branch "from the nature of its functions" would always be the "least dangerous to the political rights of the Constitution." The courts should be viewed, he argued, as "the bulwarks of a limited constitution against legislative encroachments." Their task under the new Constitution would be to "declare the sense of the law" by exercising only their judgment and never their will. This could be safely assigned to the judges for two reasons: first, they would hold neither the sword nor the purse of the country and hence would be without any real power to carry out their judgments; second, and most important, it was assumed that the Constitution would be "regarded by the judges as fundamental law,"[20] and, by a strict observance of this fundamental law, the judges would be the defenders of constitutional rights against the arts of designing men and even the factious spirit of society and would never themselves be the usurpers. Judicial independence (the main point of *Federalist*, No. 78) would enable them to safeguard the people "against the effects of [such] occasional ill humours in the society" as would be reflected in bad laws. These effects, Hamilton continued, "sometime extend no farther than to the injury of the private rights of particular classes of citizens by unjust and partial laws," and in such instances an independent judiciary is essential to "mitigating the severity and confining the operation of such laws."[21] But what would keep the judges from exercising their will rather than their judgment? Beyond a strict adherence to the Constitution as fundamental law, Hamilton looked to "strict rules and precedents" to avoid arbitrary discretion in the courts. By these rules and precedents, judges would be "bound down"; and the rules and precedents would further "serve to define and point out their duty in every particular case" that would come before them. Further, he reminded his deliberative readers, the Constitution created an emphatically limited judicial authority. This "judicial authority of the federal judicatures," he pointed out:

> is declared by the constitution to comprehend certain cases specifically specified. The expression of those cases marks the precise limits beyond which the federal courts cannot extend their jurisdiction; because the objects of their cognizance being enumerated the specification would be nugatory if it did not exclude all ideas of more extensive authority.[22]

This fact came to bear, in Hamilton's mind, upon what could be interpreted as the inclusion of a too expansive and undefined power of equity in the general grant of the judicial power. The Constitution had left to the legislature the power to constitute inferior courts and to control the appellate jurisdiction of the Supreme Court. This power, Hamilton concluded, "is a power to prescribe the mode" of the operation of those courts, and hence the legislature can be expected to exert control over such matters as jurisdictions of inferior courts.

In countering the arguments against the proposed Constitution because it failed to extend the right to a jury trial to all civil cases, Hamilton was forced to admit that he saw "great advantages" in the "separation of the equity from the law jurisdiction" in the federal courts. In particular, he thought that causes that had more of an equitable than a legal complexion would be "improperly committed to juries" because they would present questions "too complicated for a decision in that mode."[23]

Hamilton understood that the "peculiar province" of courts of equity was to offer relief from "hard bargains: these are contracts, in which, though there may have been no direct fraud or deceit, sufficient to invalidate them in a court of law; yet there may have been some undue and unconscionable advantage taken of the necessities or misfortunes of one of the parties." Such hard bargains would not be tolerated by a court of equity.[24] Most subjects of litigation "between individuals" often involve elements of "*fraud, accident, trust,* or *hardship,*" that render the suit a matter of equitable rather than legal jurisdiction.[25] And in *Federalist,* No. 83, his understanding of equitable jurisdiction is clearly revealed. "The great and primary use of a court of equity," he observed, "is to give relief in *extraordinary cases,* which are *exceptions* to general rules." In a footnote to this passage he went on to remark that "the principles by which . . . relief is governed are now reduced to a regular system, but it is not the less true that they are in the main applicable to *special* circumstances which form exceptions to general rules."[26] Thus, for Hamilton the power of equity applied to cases arising between individuals over "hard bargains," which demanded, strictly speaking, that exceptions be

41

made to the general rules. And this power was to be confined by adherence to the precedents that had evolved in equity jurisprudence. The rules of interpretation followed by judges in matters of equity, as in matters of law, were to be the "rules of common sense,"[27] whereby the spirit of the law would guide the judgment and mitigate the severity of the letter of the law.

Because the proper sphere of equity jurisdiction was still a matter of "frequent and intricate discussions"[28] and because there is "hardly a subject of litigation . . . which may not involve . . . ingredients . . . which would render the matter an object of equitable rather than of legal jurisdiction," the Framers saw the necessity of making sure that the judicial power of their new Constitution could reach to matters of both law and equity.[29] But they left to the legislature, guided as its members would be by "future lights," the more thorny problem of establishing the jurisdictional niceties of the inferior federal courts as they would relate to equity.

IV

Another leading Founder, James Wilson of Pennsylvania, had also been thoroughly versed in equity jurisprudence. The primary source of his thoughts on the subject is the series of lectures he delivered in 1790 and 1791 as the first law professor at the College of Philadelphia.[30]

The lecture in which he addressed the question of equity abounds with citations to his sources, and of special interest here is his heavy reliance on Blackstone's *Commentaries* and Kames's *Principles of Equity*. He employed his authorities to advantage and made a powerful case for dismissing as absurd any strict separation of equity from law.

For Wilson, courts of law are also courts of equity, and courts of equity must also be courts of law. The reason is clear: both questions of law and questions of equity have, as their primary object, justice. To separate the two concerns is to undermine the primary object of all judicial power. Law and equity are woven so closely together that to separate them would rip asunder the fabric of justice.

Law and equity, Wilson told his students, "are in a state of continual progression; one occupying incessantly the ground which the other, in its advancement, has left. The posts now possessed by strict law were formerly possessed by equity; and the posts now possessed by equity will hereafter be possessed by strict law." In this dialectical movement in jurisprudence, equity is the "conductor of law towards a state of refinement and perfection." Thus every court of law must also be a court of equity because "every institution should contain in it the seeds of its perfection, as well as of its preservation."[31] And, through time, this dialectical movement will push man's positive law closer to the higher demands of justice.

Wilson, like Blackstone, Kames, and Hamilton, looked at the equity power as a self-regulating phenomenon. Equity comes to be governed by "precedents and rules" no less than do courts of law.[32] This is the happy result of the nature of decrees in equity, which, "at first discretionary, will gradually be directed by general principles and rules."[33] By adhering to these precedents and rules, the judges will not indulge in equitable interpretation "rashly" and will thus remain the "ministers" and not the "arbiters" of the laws. Judges, Wilson thought, are more often than not restrained by their "reverence for a series of former concurring determinations."[34]

V

The reaction against the constitutional provision for the judicial power to extend to equity as well as to law was surprisingly limited. Most of the Anti-Federalist sentiments against the judicial branch of the new Constitution were only occasionally concerned with equity. It was, of course, duly noted that "there may be courts of Equity as well as Law,"[35] since the establishment and hence the jurisdictions of inferior courts were left to the discretion of the legislature. But the primary concern of the Anti-Federalists was the fear, loudly expressed by George Mason in the Virginia ratifying debates, that the nature of the federal judiciary was such that its "effect and operation will be utterly to destroy the state governments."[36] The question, finally, was not one of law and equity but rather whether the equity power should reside in the state, rather than the federal, judiciary.[37] Very few Anti-Federalists concerned themselves with the theoretical questions surrounding equity itself, but those who did exhibited a profound understanding of both the legal and the theoretical questions.

Robert Yates, hiding behind the pen of "Brutus," was the most thorough critic in enumerating the potential dangers of equity. The judicial power, he contended, by extending to equity, would naturally empower the courts to "explain the constitution according to the reasoning spirit of it, without being confined to the words or letter."[38] The danger of such expansive equitable interpretations he found to be strongly countenanced by the document itself. Most of the articles—especially the most powerful grants—"are conceived in general and indefinite terms, which are either equivocal, ambiguous, or which require long definitions to unfold their meaning."[39] In the course of making such equitable interpretations the judges will feel no necessity to confine themselves to "any fixed or established rules, but will determine, according to what appears to them, the reason and the spirit of the constitution." This awesome judicial power, concluded "Brutus," will move silently and imperceptibly toward completing the tendency of the proposed constitution, which he saw as the "entire subversion of the legislative, executive, and judicial powers of the individual states."[40] Finally, beyond the utter destruction of the states, he thought that equitable interpretation would facilitate extension of the federal legislative authority and lead to the gradual enlargement of the jurisdiction of all federal courts.[41]

To the contention that equity would be controlled by rules and precedents, the Anti-Federalist response was clear. In the "Letters from a Federal Farmer" (thought to be Richard Henry Lee), the writer would not be deceived by the rhetoric of the Federalists:

> It is a very dangerous thing to vest in the same judge power to decide on law, and also general powers in equity; for if the law restrain him, he is only to step into his shoes of equity, and give what judgment his reason or opinion may dictate. . . .

As for precedents, the "Farmer" continued, "we have no precedents in this country, as yet, to regulate the divisions in equity . . . ; therefore, in the supreme court for many years [equity] will be mere discretion."[42] Moreover, he argued, whatever body of precedent that might in future years accumulate would never be any more than a collection of opinions of earlier, totally unrestrained judges about what they perceived the spirit of the Constitution to be; thus, the original letter of the Constitution would ultimately be replaced by the fluctuating opinions of judges.

VI

When most of the dust stirred up by the ratification struggle had settled, and the Anti-Federalist declamations against the Constitution had been quieted somewhat by the adoption of the document, the question of the equity power was pushed from the states' ratifying conventions and from the pages of partisan newspapers into the newly elected House of Representatives and Senate. In these deliberative bodies, many of whose members had also served as members of the Convention and as ratification leaders, the debate was reopened.

In April, 1789, the Senate formed a Committee for Organizing the Judiciary, composed of Oliver Ellsworth of Connecticut, William Paterson of New Jersey, William Maclay of Pennsylvania, Caleb Strong of Massachusetts, Richard Henry Lee of Virginia, Richard Bassett of Delaware, William Few of Georgia, Paine Wingate of New Hampshire, Ralph Izard of South Carolina, and Charles Carroll of Maryland. Only three—Ellsworth, Paterson, and Strong—possessed unqualified judicial experience. Although Ellsworth assumed the leading role in the creation of the Senate's judiciary bill, it was Paterson who boasted the greatest legal familiarity with the fine points of chancery courts and equity jurisprudence.[43] On May 11 the subcommittee named to draft the bill at least included Strong, Ellsworth, and Paterson, though Maclay failed to record the names of the subcommittee.[44] The most important action of the committee, prior to the formation of the subcommittee, was to scrap the lingering Anti-Federalist position against creating new inferior federal courts; it did so by assigning the federal tasks to the existing state judicial machinery. But in order to assuage the deepest fear of the Anti-Federalists—that the federal judiciary would devour the states'—the committee moved to divide the country into federal judicial districts geographically coterminous with the existing states. The Anti-Federalist position was further considered when the committee mandated that each district-court judge was to be a resident of the district.[45]

With regard to federal equity jurisdiction, the Senate bill was a strange document indeed. It furnished implementation for the supremacy clause by permitting the use of writs of error for the review of chancery decrees and by empowering the Supreme Court to review and subsequently affirm or reverse on a petition in error any "final judgment or decree in the highest court of law or equity of a state."[46] But in section 16 the equity jurisdiction was rather severely restricted. The committee provided "that suits in equity shall not be sustained in either of the courts of the United States in any case where a remedy may be had at law."[47] The bill also outlined certain equity procedures to be used in the courts of law; for these they borrowed, in particular, the discovery procedure and methods of proof as these had been used in chancery procedure in New York and England, respectively.[48]

On the day before the bill was to be voted on, Samuel Chase (who in 1796 would be appointed an associate justice of the Supreme Court) wrote to Richard Henry Lee, expressing his thoughts on the pending bill (especially as it pertained to chancery jurisdiction). He favored both an enlargement of the chancery jurisdiction and its separation at the federal level from common-law courts. Fearing, one suspects, as the "Federal Farmer" had expressed it in the "Letters," the easy switching by judges from their shoes of law to their shoes of equity, Chase was particularly adamant on separate jurisdictions. But a cleavage between law and equity did not, as we have seen, receive popular support. Other members, Ellsworth and Maclay among them, embraced another alternative.

On July 11, on a motion by Paterson, the provision restricting equity to cases where a remedy at law was not to be had had been deleted from the pending bill. Whether this represented an effort to maintain greater fluidity in equity cases is not clear. On July 13, Ellsworth brought the subject to the fore and indicated that this provision, which had been expunged two days before, was at once necessary and sufficient as a "boundary-line between the courts of chancery and common law."[49] Maclay rose to second the motion to restore it to the bill and warned the senators that without such a provision the bill would produce "something much worse" than an independent court of chancery. "The line," he thundered, "between chancery and common law" had been broken down; the stricken provision was vital to the judicial power. Maclay's and Ellsworth's arguments in behalf of this procedural method of discrimination were persuasive. The Senate not only restored the provision but restricted equity jurisdiction even further by demanding a "plain, adequate," and "complete" remedy at law.[50] The discussion of the Senate bill in the House drew only four amendments, none of which broached the equity question. The bill was signed into law as the Judiciary Act of 1789 on September 24.

What Congress had effected was something of a balance between those who advocated a hard separation of law and equity between two courts and those who wanted equity to be a judicial tool freely usable in each court. On the one hand, the act extended equity jurisdiction to all federal courts; on the other, it established a firm rule as to when causes in equity could and could not be sustained. It also extended the appellate jurisdiction of the Supreme Court to cover equity decrees from the state courts when brought by a petition in error, thus providing federal control over equity cases in the states.

Coming on the heels of the Judiciary Act of 1789 was the Process Act of that same year, produced by the same committee that had created the Judiciary Act. The fundamental question addressed was whether the federal judicial process was to be uniform throughout the states or fragmented according to the received procedures of the then-existing states. It was, in brief, a further continuation of the Federalist–Anti-Federalist debate over consolidation. The Process Act is most significant in that its last section provided that equity proceedings follow civil law. In 1792 a new process bill was initiated; its intent was to repeal the Process Act of 1789 and the acts of 1790 and 1791 that had extended its life. The most far-reaching amendment concerned the procedure of equity.

The earlier provision, that equity procedure follow the procedure of the civil law—a strange provision—was rejected in favor of one that was even stranger. The Senate version had federal equity procedure following

the course which hath obtained in the states respectively in like causes or in states which have not courts of equity jurisdiction . . . according to the course of proceedings in such courts . . . in any adjoining or the nearest state in which they have been instituted; subject, however, to such deviations in each state by rule of courts, as a difference of circumstances may require or as may be requisite to prevent unnecessary delay and expense.[51]

The House proceeded to improve on this garbled Senate version so as to guide equity procedures simply "according to the principles, rules, and usages, which belong to a court of equity as contradistinguished from a court of common law, except so far as may have been provided" by the more fundamental Judiciary Act.[52] When this House amendment was referred back to the Senate, it was redrafted to give the Supreme Court the discretion to make alterations or additions or such regulations as it might think proper for prescribing procedure in the lower courts.[53] This bill was signed into law on May 8, 1792, and in August the chief justice of the Supreme Court, John Jay, announced that his Court would "consider the practices of the Courts of Kings Bench and Chancery in England, as affording outlines for the practice" of the Court and would "from time to time make such alterations . . . as circumstances may render necessary."[54]

The safety provided in the Judiciary Act of 1789 and the subsequent process acts rested on a rigid separation of the procedure of equity pleadings from the procedure of pleadings at law, while leaving each court with jurisdiction extending to all cases in both law and equity. The draftsmen saw this procedural distinction as necessary if equity was to be kept from becoming a dangerous source of unfettered judicial discretion.

2

The Transformation of American Equity: 1792–1954

Joseph Story   I would speak to the consciences of honorable men, and ask how they can venture, without any knowledge of existing laws, to recommend changes which may cut deep into the quick of remedial justice, or bring into peril all that is valuable in jurisprudence by its certainty, its policy, or its antiquity. Surely they need not be told, how slow every good system of laws must be in consolidating; and how easily the rashness of an hour may destroy what ages have scarcely cemented in a solid form. The oak, which requires centuries to rear its trunk, and stretch its branches, and strengthen its fibres, and fix its roots, may yet be levelled in an hour. It may breast the tempest of a hundred years, and survive the scathing of the lightning. It may even acquire vigor from its struggles with the elements, and strike its roots deeper and wider as it rises in its majesty; and yet a child, in the very wantonness of folly, may in an instant destroy it by removing a girdle of its bark.

Three The Constitution and the
Common Law in the Early Republic

As the new republic prepared to edge its way
into the nineteenth century, a debate began
over the nature of American law that was to
dominate American jurisprudence for the
next century and a half. The discussion focused on
the extent of the authority of the common-law tradition under the American Constitution. It began
with the Jeffersonian reaction to the Federalist
judiciary, continued through the efforts to codify
the common law, and ended only with the merger of
law and equity in the Rules for Civil Procedure
promulgated by the Supreme Court in 1938.
Although the formal argument was carried on
primarily in terms of the common law, it reached to
the essence of the theory of equity, and, before it
was over, it had greatly transformed the American
understanding of equity by manipulating equity
procedure.

The dialogue over the common law that began in
Jeffersonian America grew from the seed planted in
modern political philosophic discourse by Thomas
Hobbes. It is thus to Hobbes that we must first turn
our attention.

I

Hobbes's philosophic and political project was pre-
ceded in time and temperament by Niccolò
Machiavelli's "realist" revolt against the classical
tradition.[1] Machiavelli radically attacked that tradition by denying that justice has any natural support,
any superhuman support. Machiavelli took his

51

bearings not from how men ought to live but from his empirical observations of how men in fact do live their lives. The writers of antiquity had found support for human standards of justice in a nature that transcended humanity, but Machiavelli denied the possibility of such "natural" laws. Hobbes, building on this realistic basis, sought to resurrect concern for natural law. His thrust was to "maintain the idea of natural law but to divorce it from the idea of man's perfection."[2] With Hobbes, the new natural law, built on a Machiavellian foundation, took as its natural essence not the reason of man but his passions. Hobbes declared that natural law must have its foundation not simply in man's passions but in his strongest passion—the fear of violent death. Thus, in the modern tradition, natural law comes to have, as its primary object, mere life rather than a life well lived. Human virtue is replaced by human existence.

To support this new and lower conception of natural law. Hobbes was driven to construct the state-of-nature apparatus, which saw man as a radically atomistic, prepolitical, and even presocial being who entered civil society not because it fulfilled his nature (in the way the *polis* did for Aristotle) but rather because life in the state of nature tended to be "nasty, brutish, and short." Civil society, thus formed for the corporeal convenience of man, has its legitimacy not in nature but in consent.[3] With the theoretical foundation of natural law reduced from human reason to human passion, and the political foundation of civil society reduced from nature to convention, law suffered a like reduction, from an obligatory set of moral rules discovered in nature to a starkly positivistic set of rules fashioned by human consent. With this reduction of law to mere consent, the original natural-law foundation of the common-law tradition began to crumble. In order to resist the complete collapse of the common law, it was necessary to build a new foundation to replace the one destroyed by the Hobbesian assault. One of the more innovative constructions was the moral-sense theory, developed in Scotland in the late eighteenth century.

The exact influence of the Scottish moralists on American thought is impossible to measure, but we do know that, during the American Founding, such Scottish authors as Adam Smith and Adam Ferguson were widely read and discussed and frequently invoked by the proponents of the "new science of politics." In particular, James Wilson was responsible for introducing many Scottish Enlightenment theories into American political thinking. Born in Scotland and educated at St. Andrews University, Wilson came to America and became a guiding voice in the creation of the new republic. As a signer of the Declaration of Independence from Pennsylvania, as one of the leading delegates to the Philadelphia Convention (second only to Madison in his theoretical con-

tributions to the final document), as an associate justice of the United
States Supreme Court, and as professor of law in the College of Philadelphia, James Wilson's jurisprudence deserves special attention.[4]

II

During his law lectures at the College of Philadelphia in 1790–91, Wilson
delved into every aspect of jurisprudence. Of special interest to us are his
lectures "Of the Law of Nature" and "Of the Common Law," for they
give an insight into the new notion of American law.[5]

Wilson began his lecture on the law of nature by pointing out that to be
without law is disagreeable to the nature of man. Man's nature demands
restraint; it needs to be guided by fixed rules and principles of conduct so
that men and societies will not become the sports of "the fierce gusts of
passion, and the fluctuating billows of caprice."[6] There is, he assured his
students, a moral obligation by which men are bound. There are natural
rules and principles by which we are obligated to order our lives. But
how, given the blow dealt human reason by the epistemological assumptions of Hobbes, is this to be achieved? Wilson posed his reply in a series
of questions and answers:

> Having thus stated the question—what is the efficient cause of moral
> obligation?—I gave it this answer—the will of God.... If I am
> asked—why do you obey the will of God? I answer—because it is my
> duty to do so. If I am asked again—how do you know this to be your
> duty? I answer again—because I am told so by my moral sense or
> conscience. If I am asked a third time—how do you know that you
> ought to do that, of which your conscience enjoins the performance? I
> can only say, I *feel* such is my duty. Here investigation must stop;
> reasoning can go no farther.[7]

This moral sense that allows men to "know" right from wrong is in human
nature and "has been felt and acknowledged in all ages and nations."[8]
Man's judgment as to right and wrong is intuitive rather than rational; his
moral judgment is, in the strictest meaning of the term, a "common
sense"[9] shared by all men, regardless of their rational skills. All first
principles of human virtue are thus written on the hearts of men "in
characters so legible that no man can pretend ignorance of them or of his
obligation to practice them."[10]

Wilson saw, however, a distinct and necessary place for human reason
in the natural scheme of things. The conscience or moral sense of man
determines only his ends; "the means of attaining this end must be determined by reason," and it is in the selection of means that problems
arise:

> To select and ascertain those means, is often a matter of very considerable difficulty. Doubts may arise; opposite interests may occur; and a preference must be given to one side from a small over-balance, and from very nice views. This is particularly the case in questions with regard to justice.[11]

Given man's fallible reasoning and the insufficiency of human wisdom to know justice, the common law, in Wilson's view, was a necessary complement to man's political condition, for "what we call human reason, in general, is not so much the knowledge, or experience, or information of any one man, as the knowledge and experience, and information of many, arising from lights mutually and successively communicated and improved." The common law, Wilson insisted, "like natural philosophy ... is a science founded on experiment."[12] He saw it as the sum of the different efforts made by men through time to understand and commit to general rules the complex relationships that exist between human beings in their political situation. Its authority derived from "reception, approbation [and] custom, long and established."[13] This authority rested ultimately on consent, for consent is "the true origin of the obligation in human laws."[14] Custom is only "intrinsick evidence of consent."[15] The common law was introduced by "voluntary adoption," was made general by "the instances of voluntary adoption being increased," and became lasting by the "voluntary and satisfactory experience, which ratified and confirmed what voluntary adoption had introduced."[16]

Unlike natural law, the common law is mutable. The consent on which it rests is also capable of changing, enlarging, improving, and repealing the common law. As society changes, the common law must change to reflect the "circumstances, the exigencies, and the conveniences of the people by whom it is appointed."[17]

Wilson's lectures reflect the fact that by the end of the eighteenth century Americans had begun to offer a new foundation for the common law. No longer seen to rest on the old natural-law foundation, the common law was viewed as resting on consent expressed in the form of custom and continued usage. "The result of this transformation in the underlying basis for the legitimacy of the common law was that jurists began to conceive of the common law as an instrument of will."[18] The judiciary, seeing that they derived their power from the same source as the legislature (i.e., the people), began to "think of the common law as equally responsible with legislation for governing society and promoting socially desirable conduct."[19] By the early nineteenth century, the effects of common-law judgments had taken on many of the qualities of legislation.[20] The reaction of the Jeffersonian Republicans to this new judicial attitude was strong.

III

The great burst of Republican resistance to the Federalists' presumption that the jurisdiction of the federal judiciary embraced the common-law tradition did not occur until 1798–99. It came as a response to the hated Alien and Sedition Acts.[21] Their resistance was a principled one, however, and not simply the result of partisan political zeal. The Jeffersonian Republican argument was rooted firmly in the earlier thought of the party's great theoreticians, Thomas Jefferson and James Madison.

As early as 1776 Jefferson had expressed to Edmund Pendleton his view that a judge should be a "mere machine," without authority to dispense with laws that had been produced by a properly instituted representative legislature.[22] As his commitment to an emphatically limited government matured, it continued to embrace the idea of a strictly limited judiciary. A judiciary granted too much flexibility or too great a jurisdiction was inconsistent with the genius of republican government.[23]

When the delegates convened in Philadelphia in the summer of 1787, James Madison took with him a view of the common law he shared with Jefferson, his friend and fellow Virginian. On August 17, during a debate over the proposed power of the legislature "to declare the law and punishment of piracies and felonies," Madison objected to James Wilson's observation that "felonies" were "sufficiently defined by Common Law."[24] To Madison, the standard of "felony at common law" was not only "vague" but also "defective." He went beyond the specific felony issue at hand and addressed the broader question of the place of the common law under the Constitution. No foreign law, he insisted, "should be a standard farther than is expressly adopted." Recurrence to the common law as a general standard for defining the specifics of the new document would secure neither "uniformity nor stability in the law." The "proper remedy" for the confusion that would be generated by a common-law standard would be to "vest the power proposed by the term 'define' in the Natl. legislature." Madison's motion to give the legislature the power to define "felony" was passed.[25]

Madison later elaborated his views on the place of the common law under the pending Constitution in response to George Mason's objection that the Constitution failed to secure to the people the "enjoyment and benefit of the common law."[26] In a letter of October 18, 1787, to George Washington, Madison confessed that he was at a loss to comprehend what Mason meant by the objection.[27] In particular, Madison addressed Mason's contention that the common law had been adopted by the states. "The common law," Madison argued, "is nothing more than the unwritten law, and is left by all the [state] constitutions equally liable to legislative alterations." If, in fact, the state constitutions mentioned the common law specifically (a point Madison doubted), he was sure it was nothing more than a "general declaration" that it would continue in force until changed. The Constitution of Virginia, which had been "drawn up by Col. Mason himself," Madison reminded Washington, was "absolutely silent on the subject." Turning from the constitutions of the states to the proposed national Constitution, Madison pointed out that the Convention could not possibly have incorporated the common law into the new document. At the very least, such an action "would have broken in upon the legal code of every state in the most material points"; at the very worst, such an incorporation "would have brought over from G[reat] B[ritain] a thousand heterogeneous & anti-republican doctrines, and even the *ecclesiastical hierarchy itself,* for that is a part of the common law." If, instead of incorporating wholesale the vagaries of the common law, the Convention had attempted to discriminate those parts applicable to America, the result would have been a "digest of laws instead of a Constitution."

Jefferson and Madison apparently considered the relationship of the common law to the Constitution to have been settled, but in 1798 the Federalist-sponsored Alien and Sedition Acts served notice that the debate was being resumed. The political circumstances that gave rise to the acts were painful enough, but their theoretical implications were seen by the Republicans as striking at the heart of the republican liberty of the Constitution. Beyond the more obvious problems the Alien and Sedition Acts presented to the Bill of Rights, they were being justified by the Federalists on the basis of the common law, which they held had been carried over even after the Constitution had been ratified. In response to this assertion the Republican voices joined in a clear and absolute denial.

The leading Republican spokesman in the congressional debates in 1798 over the sedition bill was Albert Gallatin. Powerfully presenting the Republican position in an attempt to halt the Federalist offensive, he directly attacked the constitutional interpretation offered by the Massachusetts Federalist Harrison Gray Otis. The Federalists insisted that the sedition bill was constitutional on two grounds: first, although it was not a specifically delegated power, Congress had the authority to reach seditious libel through the necessary-and-proper clause; second, and even more aggravating to Republican sensibilities, Otis claimed that the "Constitution granted the federal courts common law jurisdiction over criminal cases, including sedition." Otis went beyond mere implication and proclaimed that Article III of the Constitution explicitly conferred common-law jurisdiction on the federal courts by providing that the judicial power should extend to all "cases arising under the constitution." Since this clearly meant something besides mere statutes, Otis concluded that "cases arising under the constitution" were in fact cases arising under the common law, "that legal discretion which had been exercised in England since time immemorial." He further supported his thesis by turning to examples of the specific language of the Constitution—"jury," "trial," "impeachment"—which, he insisted, could be defined only by the common law. Therefore, the Constitution had unmistakably intended the federal judiciary to have common-law jurisdiction.[28]

Gallatin's response was sharp and to the point. He first pointed out that Otis' argument was contradictory: if, in fact, the Constitution provided for jurisdiction over common-law sedition, then no statute was necessary. The insistence of the Federalists in favor of such a statute revealed their own implicit recognition of the shaky constitutional foundation on which they stood. Gallatin went further and denied in toto the Federalist claim that Article III specifically granted jurisdiction over common-law crimes. The language of Article III, rather than being expansive, was restrictive; by clearly outlining the nature of the cases that would properly fall within the purview of the federal judicial power, the Constitution specifically excluded the common-law jurisdiction. Though recurrence to the common law to define the objects that fell within the federal jurisdiction could no doubt be anticipated, Gallatin continued, using common-law terms for definitions was a far cry from conceding an expansive common-law jurisdiction.[29]

The Republican position was clear: Congress had no authority under the Constitution or the Bill of Rights to pass laws punishing seditious libel, nor did the judiciary have jurisdiction over such common-law crimes. The Republicans reminded their opponents that under the federal scheme of the Constitution the people were under two distinct governments. Whether the states had adopted the common law and were allowed to pass sedition laws was a question beyond the present debate; what was certain was that the federal government could not.[30] Gallatin's glowing Republican rhetoric was in vain. The Federalist-dominated Congress passed the Sedition Act in 1798.

In August, 1799, Thomas Jefferson shared his animadversions on the common-law problem with Edmund Randolph. "Of all the doctrines which have ever been broached by the federal government, the novel one, of the common law being in force & cognizable as an existing law in their courts, is to me the most formidable." Jefferson continued with his indictment of what he viewed as the Federalists' perversion of the Constitution:

> All their other assumptions of un-given powers have been in the detail.
> The bank law, the treaty doctrine, the sedition act, alien act, the
> undertaking to change the state laws of evidence in the state courts by

certain parts of the stamp act . . . have been solitary, unconsequential, timid things, in comparison with the audacious, barefaced, and sweeping pretention to a system of law for the US, without the adoption of their legislature, and so infinitely beyond their power to adopt.[31]

Jefferson's vigorous denunciation of the Federalists' position on the common-law question was in response to a set of "Notes on the Common Law" Randolph had written and shared with his fellow Virginians.[32] Randolph had posed a series of questions to provide the framework of his inquiry. His general theme was "Is the Common Law of England the Law of the United States?" From this main question Randolph derived a series of "subordinate questions," which inquired into such matters as whether the common law might be the law of the United States from "the *nature* of the federal constitution" or from "a *special* adoption in the federal constitution"; whether the legislature possessed "an authority to adopt the criminal part of the common law"; and whether the judicial power of the federal Constitution extended to common-law jurisdiction in matters both criminal and civil.

Randolph concluded that the common law was "not adopted by the constitution, either from its nature or specially." As far as congressional authority over criminal common-law adoption went, Randolph found that, in executing the powers delegated to it by the Constitution, it could certainly "borrow provisions from the common law" or even from British statutes or any foreign laws. "But," he hastened to add, "it is one thing to accommodate the regulations of the common law to crimes or misdemeanors, over which a constitutional jurisdiction is already vested in Congress, and another totally different to make the common law the parent of jurisdiction in Congress over crimes and misdemeanors in which no constitutional jurisdiction is vested in Congress." Concerning the question whether the judicial jurisdiction extended over common-law crimes and misdemeanors not embraced by the Constitution or by special legislative adoption, Randolph argued that the "negative of this question" was "uncontrovertible." The use of the common law for "furnishing definitions or rules of construction or proceedings" Randolph saw as more acceptable. If Congress should choose to use common-law terms in the exercise of its powers over constitutional subjects, then the "Books of the common law . . . being not only books of common sense but also as familiar to the states," would undeniably be the "best vocabulary of definition." In establishing rules of procedure for the legislatively created inferior tribunals of the federal judiciary, Congress was free to adopt "the common law forms or any others more agreeable to them."

The general conclusion Randolph reached was that the common law could not "supply to the federal courts a source of...jurisdiction" that went beyond what the Constitution had "definitely given or what may be necessary and proper to carry those definitive powers into execution." But it could, at the pleasure of the legislature, be received in the federal courts as a means of "furnishing definitions or rules of construction or proceedings."

Jefferson objected to only one of Randolph's reflections. Randolph had asserted that the laws are "emanations" of the legislative will "and when once enacted continue in force, because it is presumed to be the legislative will that they should so continue until it is otherwise promulgated." To Jefferson it was important to emphasize that it is the "will of the nation which makes the law obligatory; it is their will which creates or annihilates the organ which is to declare and announce it."[33] Aside from the objection expressed in this one clarifying response, Jefferson held Randolph's work to be generally estimable, and he proceeded to share further his own views on the same topic.

To assume that common law had been incorporated in the Constitution, Jefferson held, was not only a dangerous assumption; it was logically flawed. The law of the United States could not precede in time the establishment of the United States; the law became law only after there were "organs" established for declaring that law. Therefore, "the common law did not become, ipso facto, law on the new association; it could only become so by a positive adoption, & so far only as they were authorized to adopt."[34] The danger posed by the Federalist assertions was real and immediate for Jefferson and the Republicans. He believed that, "if the principle were to prevail, of a common law being in force in the U.S., (which principle possesses the general government at once of all the powers of the state governments and reduces us to a single and consolidated government,) it would become the most corrupt government on the earth."[35]

The Republican defense was strongly constitutional. The republic created by the Constitution had as its end political liberty; the preservation of that liberty depended on strict adherence to the letter of the document. To proclaim that the common law hovered over the republic as an omnipotent spirit, ready to be invoked at will by Congress or the courts, was to proclaim the undesirability of an emphatically limited national government and to encourage the gradual consolidation of the states into one republic. The idea of a consolidated republic was still, in 1798, viewed by Jefferson and Madison as politically "inexpedient."[36] To preserve liberty, it was necessary to preserve the Constitution inviolate. The common-law arguments of the Federalists would stretch the Constitution into something its framers never intended, injecting into it the uncertain spirit of English forms of jurisprudence. In such circumstances, the law would depend, not on the stable and fixed provisions of the Constitution, but only on the fluctuating and uncertain opinions of judges. Republicans could not accept this interpretation.

Republican antipathy to the Federalist position reached its most polished and forceful expression in the Virginia and Kentucky Resolutions. In the Virginia report James Madison cogently addressed the common-law question, tracing with care the political history of the United States. Neither colonial history nor the Articles of Confederation could be found to support the "extraordinary doctrine" being put forth by the Federalists.[37] Turning to the Constitution itself, Madison observed that "particular parts of the common law may have a sanction from the Constitution so far as they are necessarily comprehended in the technical phrases which express the powers delegated to the government," but, beyond that, there was no possibility that the common law had been incorporated.[38] Indeed, had the common law been admitted as a legal or constitutional obligation, it would have conferred "on the judicial department a discretion little short of a legislative power."[39] Madison concluded his observations on the common-law argument by noting that his committee felt "the utmost confidence in concluding that the common law never was, nor by any fair construction ever can be, deemed a law for the American people as one community." He continued:

> It is, indeed, distressing to reflect that it ever should have been made a question, whether the Constitution, on the whole face of which is seen so much labor to enumerate and define the several objects of federal power, could intend to introduce in the lump, in an indirect manner, and by a forced construction of a few phrases, the vast and multifarious jurisdiction involved in the common law—a law overspreading the entire field of legislation; and a law that would sap the foundation of the Constitution as a system of limited and specified powers. A severer reproach could not . . . be thrown on the Constitution, on those who framed, or on those who established it, than such a supposition would throw on them.[40]

This sweeping denial by Madison, the chief theoretician of the Constitution, was no mere display of partisanship; it was totally consistent with the view he had expressed during the Philadelphia Convention in 1787.

In the end, Madison and the Republicans prevailed on the issue of the Alien and Sedition laws; but their victory did not settle completely the debate over the place of the common law in American jurisprudence, and, by the 1820s, in an attempt to render the legal process less subjective and hence less political, a movement to codify the common law in the states began to gather momentum. The Codification Movement was a curious thing, fired by a strange mixture of motives that were often quite contradictory. Charles Warren suggested that, basically, five factors formed the foundation of the codifiers' motives.[41] He cited (1) a continuing hostility to all things English; (2) a distrust and jealousy of lawyers who became ensconced in positions of power because of the abstruse quality of the law; (3) the massive accumulation of law reports; (4) the influence of the Napoleonic Code; and (5) the theoretical support offered the proponents by the writings of Jeremy Bentham. Generally, the participants in the movement to codify the common law shared a fundamental faith that it was "full of metaphysical abstractions, scholastic subtilties[,] arbitrary distinctions, and intangible or incorporeal rights to things, separate from the things themselves."[42]

Particularly significant in Warren's list of motives for understanding the theoretical foundations of the Codification Movement is the work of Jeremy Bentham. Bentham was the Utilitarian par excellence; he was quite willing to "wipe the slate clean" and write complete codes of new law based on his faith in the concept of providing the greatest good for the greatest number.[43] He came to be viewed by many Americans (who, of course, for the most part were not as extreme) as "the most profound and original of law reformers."[44] With American modifications (specifically, the rejection of any attempt at complete codification), Bentham's logic began to find avid supporters among the enthusiasts of codification.

The object of the movement was to seek the depoliticization of the law and thus achieve greater certainty in the administration of justice. Given the new view that the common law was an instrument of the popular will and no longer the expression of some transcendent natural law, it seemed only appropriate that the uncertainty of the common law should be reduced by removing its subjectivity and replacing it with clearly determined objective codes. The basic impetus of the Codification Movement was the desire for simplification so that the law "might be understood by laymen as well as by specifically trained and specially favored members of the bar."[45] As the movement gained support, there arose within the ranks of the legal profession a reaction against drastic codification.

In the 1820s and 1830s America gave birth to its own "treatise tradition" of law. The main thrust of this "treatise tradition," which started in 1819 with the publication of John Milton Goodenow's *Historical Sketches of the Principles and Maxims of American Jurisprudence,* was to reduce the vagaries and varieties of the common law (generally embraced in one form or another by the states) to some systematic form. It has been argued that this was a period in which law came to be equated with "science," and the treatise tradition was the beginning of a scientific legal tradition in America.[46] But it must be remembered that a "science" of law in the early nineteenth century was a long way from what a "science" of law might mean today. Indeed, as Joseph Story's writings make clear, scientific jurisprudence was in fact a reaction against the extreme positivism of the Codification Movement and an attempt to retain some understanding of the place of natural law in American law. The treatise-writers generally were concerned with preserving more flexibility in the law than strict codification would ever allow. Their purpose was to reduce the confusion, ambiguity, and arbitrariness of the legal process by establishing standard sources and thus to undermine the main complaint of the proponents of codification. The object of most treatise-writers was to plead for a proper place for the common law under the Constitution.

IV

The chief target of the earliest treatise-writers was the doctrine of common-law crimes that, two decades earlier, had been embodied in the Alien and Sedition Acts. In the controversy that had then raged between the Federalists and the Republicans, the issue had been federal jurisdiction over common-law crimes; but, as mentioned earlier, an influential book, published in 1819, sliced through the practical arguments of federalism to attack the theoretical assumption that common-law crimes were cognizable anywhere, even in the states' judiciaries.

That book was *Historical Sketches of the Principles and Maxims of American Jurisprudence.*[47] In it, John Milton Goodenow attempted to persuade his readers of the futility of trying to understand criminal law on the basis of the old natural-law theory of abstract justice. Although human compacts can never "destroy or abrogate the principles of natural law," Goodenow insisted, "*these* may be disregarded and lie for ages buried beneath the rubbish of human invention." Human laws are merely the product of "fleshly wisdom" and are in no way bound by "the pure impulse of nature and the philosophy of man's reason." His jurisprudence, clearly the child of the modern conception of natural law, was based fully on the notion of popular consent. He endeavored to leave no doubt as to his positivist approach:

> Hence, we discover, that as the laws which man creates for himself, in his social state, are not the emanations of DIVINE WILL, nor yet the pure institutions of nature and reason; but changeable and arbitrary in their formation; they are necessarily of a *positive, local existence;* made, declared and *published* in a shape and character clear and unequivocal to all to whom they are directed; otherwise they could never

become obligatory: because they are not of intuition, discoverable by the eye of reason.[48]

Since Goodenow's view of the law was Hobbesian, he refused (unlike James Wilson) to accept any notion of a binding "moral sense." For Goodenow the problem grew from man's imperfect nature: "his reason is imperfect, and his soul is drawn from the path of rectitude by the imperceptible allurements of humanity."[49] Each man enjoys a different perception of the word of God and the law of nature; and until such time as "all shall reason and act alike, and in perfect conformity with the will of God and the laws of man's nature," there will always be the necessity of "social government and laws." Lest one think that such a day of quiet rectitude might dawn, Goodenow hastened to add that such a "day can never happen while humanity is possessed of the blood of Adam."[50] He then moved quickly to deny broad judicial discretion to those who would fill the benches of the criminal tribunals:

> The judge ... of a criminal tribunal, is *governed* himself by *positive law,* and executes and enforces the will of the supreme power, which is the will of THE PEOPLE, in their aggregate capacity.... The will of the people, or the supreme governor, he can only know when it is declared, for until then it can be no *rule* while ever that will by which a citizen is to be tried, condemned and executed, is yet secret and unknown, it is the very soul of despotism, whether it be consistent or not with reason and justice, or with the policy of the state.[51]

It is strange that, after such a vigorous attack against the notion of common-law jurisdiction in criminal actions, Goodenow then moved to exclude civil actions from his attack. *"Civil actions,"* he believed, "are founded in the private rights and wrongs of individuals," and the foundation of all private rights is "Natural justice and right reason." Natural justice and reason he found to be the "same in all countries and in all ages," and claims of private rights have no reference to the "positive expression of the public will ... because the social state depends in no way, for its safety, peace, or preservation, upon these matters of individual and private controversy."[52] In civil actions, "abstract justice and equity should be the rule of decision."[53]

The major flaw in Goodenow's argument is that, quite often, private disputes have a direct relation to the positive decrees of the public will. Certainly property laws, inheritance laws, and so forth are no more emanations of a divine will than criminal statutes are. Therefore, the strong case Goodenow presented against common-law criminal jurisdiction was equally applicable to common-law civil jurisdiction. His assault on

63

abstract principles of justice as a foundation for criminal law is, by association, an assault against their use as the foundation for civil law. The attack on natural law is also an attack on natural equity, and the resulting problem admitted of only one solution if Goodenow's logic was followed: the formalization of civil-law jurisdiction, especially of equity, into a science of equity rooted in the notion of consent rather than nature. This solution involved a new understanding of equity, one that not only lent itself to but demanded a "science," a body of equity law based on precedents reflecting popular consent from time immemorial. This view of the civil common-law jurisdictions implicit in Goodenow's work was left to be drawn out by those coming after him.

In 1824, Peter S. DuPonceau, provost of the Law Academy of Philadelphia, delivered a valedictory address that was later published as *A Dissertation on the Nature and Extent of the Jurisdiction of the Courts of the United States*.[54] During his study of the question of common-law jurisdiction, DuPonceau corresponded with James Madison and sent to him a copy of his *Dissertation*. In August, 1824, Madison wrote to DuPonceau and repeated the position he had held for nearly forty years. The great constitutional theoretician of American republicanism instructed DuPonceau that

> A characteristic peculiarity of the Gov't. of the U. States is, that its powers consist of special grants taken from the general mass of power, whereas other Gov'ts. possess the general mass with special exceptions only. Such being the plan of the Constitution, it cannot well be supposed that the body which framed it with so much deliberation, and with so manifest a purpose of specifying its objects and defining its boundaries, would, if intending that the common law should be a part of the national code have omitted to express or distinctly indicate the intention; when so many far inferior provisions are so carefully inserted, and such appears to have been the public view taken of the Instrument, whether we recur to the period of its ratification by the States, or to the federal practice under it.[55]

DuPonceau's position in the *Dissertation* was distinctly Madisonian in spirit, although Madison interpreted the book as more indulgent of the common law than he wished. DuPonceau viewed the great tradition of English common law to be "from its very nature uncertain and fluctuating," and, as such, not acceptable in America, where political institutions no longer depended upon "uncertain traditions, but on the more solid foundation of express written compacts."[56] He saw the place of the common-law tradition in America as Madison had in the Virginia Report: it was to be referred to only occasionally, for the "interpretation of pas-

sages ... which have been expressed in its well known phraseology."[57]
It was this distinction that DuPonceau endeavored to elaborate in his
Dissertation.

To assume a broad common-law jurisdiction for the judiciary, DuPonceau argued, was incompatible with American constitutionalism; for to
grant the judges such a power was tantamount to giving them an "almost
unlimited authority over the lives and fortunes of the citizens" and would
"impair, if not destroy, the sovereignty of the States, which the Constitution had meant to preserve, and even had guaranteed."[58] DuPonceau
clearly stated his project to his law students:

> The distinction which I have assumed between the common law as a
> *source* of power and as a *means* for its exercise is the foundation of
> my argument. From the common law considered in the first point of
> view, I contend that in this country no jurisdiction can arise, while in
> the second every lawful jurisdiction may be exercised through its in-
> strumentality, and by means of its proper application.[59]

DuPonceau feared to a greater degree than Madison, however, the loss
of the common law as a "system of jurisprudence" in favor of the less
"malleable" written codes and statutes. He believed that Americans lived
"in the midst of the common law," that they inhaled "it at every breath"
and "imbibed it at every pore." He saw the common law as being "interwoven with the very idiom that we speak." It would be impossible, he
insisted, to learn another system of laws "without learning at the same
time another language." Americans could not even "think of right or of
wrong but through the medium of the ideas that they had derived from
the common law,"[60] and, should the justices of the Supreme Court ever
deny by decree the underlying presence of the common law, "they would
not have the power to carry this decision into effect, & the common law
would still govern tho' under another name." DuPonceau's position was
to admit the common law "at once as the foundation of ... American
Jurisprudence, (except as to conferring power, which the Constitution &
laws alone can do) & to endeavour to give it a right direction."[61] Con-
fessing that he was aware that the common law had "been abused to
subserve party views," DuPonceau insisted that such abuse could be
avoided if the common law could be seen as the foundation for "Republican & liberal principles." If these principles could come to dominate
the American legal mind, then the common law would assume a "proper
shape." Denial of the legitimacy of the common law in American jurisprudence would not prevent abuses from creeping in; in fact, such abuses
could perhaps "creep in more easily ... without the common law than
with it."[62]

The problem with drastic codification was that such "codes would be formed from the same elements which compose the common law, and would exhibit the same defects," but they would no longer be susceptible of gradual improvement. Once codified, the common law would possess all the "unbending imperative force of statutory enactments." The alternative was to "methodise" the common law in order to raise it to its "highest degree of perfection" and preserve the "excellent principles" with which it was fraught.[63] In short, the common law had to be treated as a "philosophical science,"[64] and to do this required the careful and slow elaboration of its sound principles, for "nothing is uniform but sound principles."[65] To allow the common law to remain a series of unconnected decrees would be to lessen its dignity and make the greatest lawyer the one with the "strongest habitual or artificial memory."

DuPonceau ended his *Dissertation* with a plea to the legal profession to begin to reflect on the subject by "learned treatises and free discussions" so that the "true principles of jurisprudence" would begin to "take root in the minds of the members of the legal profession" itself.[66] It appears that his plea was heeded, for in a few years law libraries began to be stuffed with "learned treatises." America's treatise tradition was about to burst into full bloom.

In 1826 James Kent published the first of the four volumes of his *Commentaries on American Law*.[67] Unlike the earlier writers, who had more or less dabbled with various aspects of American jurisprudence, Kent's project was an exhaustive treatment of American law, incorporating not only court decisions but treatises as well, both American and English. The effort was so exemplary of the new American attitude toward the law that George Bancroft was led to remark, "Now we know what American Law is; we know it is a science."[68] Kent also addressed the common-law-jurisdiction question, but his remarks largely derived from his basic agreement with DuPonceau's conclusions. He did attempt to refine, somewhat, the argument as to why the common law was a "necessary and safe guide" for the exercise of the jurisdictions granted by the Constitution and by subsequent legislation. It could be seen as providing some pattern to judicial decision-making; after all, the essence of the common law was precedent, and there was a certain safety achieved by a religious adherence to precedent. "Without such a guide," Kent concluded, "the courts would be left to a dangerous discretion, and to roam at large in the trackless field of their own imaginations."[69] In America, Kent assured his students, the common law, "under the benign influence of an expanded commerce, of enlightened justice, of republican principles, and a sound philosophy, [had] become a code of matured ethics, and enlarged civil wisdom, admirably adapted to promote and secure the freedom and happiness of social life."[70]

Kent also assumed the task of providing something of a source book of common-law authorities, and he recommended that not only the reports of adjudged cases should be consulted but "numerous other works of sages in the profession," whose efforts would "contribute very essentially to facilitate the researches, and abridge the labour of the student."[71] Among the authorities he suggested were the masters of English jurisprudence: Glanville's *De Legibus Angliae*, Bracton's *De Legibus et Consuetudinibus Angliae*, St. Germain's *Dialogues*, Fortesque's *De Laudibus Legum Angliae*, Bacon's *Elements of the Common Law*, Coke's *Institutes*, and Blackstone's *Commentaries*. It was his firm conviction that American lawyers should not forget the legitimate parentage of their common-law tradition.

Kent had a balanced view of the advantages and disadvantages of efforts to codify the law in all its minutiae. He believed, with Sir Matthew Hale, that the common law was the product of the "wisdom, counsel, experience, and observation, of many ages of wise and observing men." He saw a dangerous tendency in those "bold projectors who can think of striking off a perfect code of law at a single essay."[72] On the other hand, he recognized that the evils resulting from an "indigestible heap of laws, and legal authorities," were also "great and manifest." He was willing to admit that the "spirit of the present age, and the cause of truth and justice," required more simplicity in the system of law, but not at the price of the complete annihilation of the common law. The common law was a vital part of any legal system; it could be clarified by codification where appropriate, but only where appropriate, and not to the degree that it would lose its flexibility to "meet with various emergencies."[73]

After the last volume of Kent's *Commentaries* appeared in 1830, the treatise-writers produced volume after volume on all aspects of the law. In 1832 James Gould published *A Treatise on the Principles of Pleading*, in which he sought to offer *"instruction in the science of pleading"* and to show that the doctrines of pleading were not merely a "compilation of *positive rules"* but rather formed a "system of *consistent and rational principles,* adapted, with the utmost precision, to the administration of justice."[74] Gould found himself in complete agreement with Lord Coke, who had characterized pleading as "the *truest guide* to the knowledge of the common law."[75] His effort was aimed at salvaging a place for human rationality in the law:

For while every other science is taught, by a detailed explication of its *principles*, the doctrines of the common law are usually exhibited, in our legal treatises, as if they were the insulated enactments of *positive law*—without reference to the *reasons* on which they rest. And thus the common law is presented, in most of our books, rather as an *art*, than a science; and the acquisition of it made to depend, more upon the mechanical strength of the reader's *memory*, than upon the exercise of his *understanding*.[76]

Not all legal writers of this period aimed solely at the professional audience. It was part of the faith that simplification of the law was also needed by laymen. In 1835 Francis Hilliard designed his text, *The Elements of Law*, as "a cheap manual for popular use."[77] His purpose was to offer for public consumption a compendium of the "broad and fixed principles" of the science of law, which "remain unchanged amidst the fluctuations of successive ages." The vast increase in the body of legal pronouncements, Hilliard thought, did not reflect any change in the fundamental principles but only "the infinite variety of facts and circumstances, to which the transactions of mankind give rise." In spite of this mass of details, there remained only a "few comprehensive, elementary maxims, of which those details are merely the occasional modification." Hilliard attempted to extract those maxims of general truth and applicability and thus relieve the confusion in the public mind that held the law to be at once infinite and obscure.[78]

Hilliard contended that the law of the land did indeed reflect the law of nature. Municipal laws, he argued, had no other foundation than "equity, reason, and right."[79] What he sought to bring into public vision were not mere positive decrees but rather "natural" maxims of the law, which had come to be known through the long train of human experience. Although less well known than some of the other treatises, Hilliard's little book is one of the clearest expressions of the purpose generally sought by the other authors: to clear away the confusion surrounding the law, not by a strict reduction to rigid codes, but by elaborating the fundamental principles of the law as these had developed through the ages. The treatise-writers of the 1820s and 1830s can be accused of seeking a *science* of law only if one means by this a modified philosophic rather than an extremely positivistic science. Their concern was to retain the vitality of a notion of justice beyond simple positive decrees, and their effort to reduce the law to order was not an effort to emasculate the common law's concern for standards of natural justice but to preserve as much of that tradition as they could in the face of a growing popular distrust and animosity toward a system of law that had not always been put to noble use.

Among the eminent men who contributed to the American treatise tradition, one stands far above the rest. By his astonishing prolificacy and erudition, Joseph Story clearly surpasses the others. Between 1832 and

1845 he produced exhaustive commentaries on nearly every aspect of American jurisprudence: *Commentaries on Bailments* (1832); *Commentaries on the Constitution of the United States,* in three volumes (1833); *Commentaries on the Conflict of Laws* (1834); *Commentaries on Equity Jurisprudence,* in two volumes (1836); *Commentaries on Equity Pleading* (1838); *Commentaries on Agency* (1839); *Commentaries on Partnership* (1841); *Commentaries on Bills of Exchange* (1843); and *Commentaries on Promissory Notes* (1845). These were written while Story served simultaneously as Dane Professor of Law at Harvard and as associate justice of the United States Supreme Court (which still included circuit-riding)—a remarkable legacy, to say the least.

Of all Story's efforts, however, his *Commentaries on Equity Jurisprudence* is generally considered to be his masterpiece. In it he argued that equity "must have a place in every rational system of jurisprudence." The enthusiasm for codification must not be allowed to stamp out the tradition of equity; for no code, "however minute and particular," could ever provide for the "infinite variety of human affairs" and furnish rules to cover them all.[80] Justice needed equity jurisprudence; and equity jurisprudence, if it was to retain a vital place in American law, was in need of greater order. It was a formidable achievement to be able to give a degree of order—any degree of order—to that most fluid field of jurisprudence. Story's contribution to the great tradition of equity jurisprudence earned for him the regard of his profession as the father of American equity. And well it should have; for with Story we have America's most original contribution to the long tradition of equity: a philosophic "science" of equity.

Four Joseph Story's "Science" of Equity

Joseph Story's jurisprudence grew not only from a particular theoretical point of view but also as a response to the politics of his day. Together these forces wrought an understanding of the common law that demanded preservation of that branch of jurisprudence most closely related to the transcendent realm of natural law—equity. In the face of the growing democratic impulse and the effort to codify the common law, Story attempted to fashion a philosophic scheme, or "science," of equity that would be able to resist the radically positivistic demands of the codifiers. To understand Story's equity jurisprudence, one must first consider both the philosophic and practical influences that shaped his view of the common law, of which he saw equity as a branch.

I

The sea of national politics into which Joseph Story was launched in 1811 by his appointment to the United States Supreme Court was rough and choppy with democratic undercurrents. Jefferson had relinquished the presidency to James Madison in 1809, preserving the Republican occupancy. The theoretical leadership of the Federalists, which had passed from Hamilton to Marshall in 1804, continued to rest securely in the nation's highest court.

When Associate Justice William Cushing died in 1810, Jefferson rejoiced at the prospect of gaining a Republican hold in the Court as well as the presidency. He warned his fellow Republicans that it

70

was necessary to proceed with great caution in choosing the right replacement; for to find a man with "firmness enough to preserve his independence on the same Bench with Marshall" was no mean task.[1] As a possible Republican nominee, Jefferson was convinced that Joseph Story was a poor choice. He found him to be not only "too young," but, worse, he believed him to be "unquestionably a tory."[2] Madison, following Jefferson's advice, looked elsewhere, but without success. His first choice, Levi Lincoln, was confirmed but refused to serve for reasons of poor health; his second choice, Alexander Walcott, was rejected by the Senate as being unqualified; and his third choice, John Quincy Adams (an admitted foe of Blackstonian jurisprudence), also refused the appointment in order to continue in his diplomatic post. Madison, in apparent desperation, then selected the thirty-two-year-old Story, a lawyer from Salem, Massachusetts, making him the youngest man ever to serve on the Supreme Court.[3]

From Jefferson's point of view, Story proved to be even more disappointing than he had ever imagined. Not only was Story a student of Mansfield and Blackstone, both of whom Jefferson held in utter contempt as "tories," but he became Marshall's right hand on the Court. As has been observed, "Marshall himself could not have appointed a more congenial ally,"[4] for Joseph Story soon proved himself to be a strong nationalist, with marked Federalist sympathies.

Beyond his close personal and professional ties to Marshall and his fondness for Blackstone and Mansfield, Story's ardent nationalism was fired by another and more subtle force. He believed that the growing force of the democratic social and intellectual undercurrents in America was beginning to erode the foundations on which the Constitution and its regime rested. He feared that "the spirit of the age [had] broken loose from the strong ties, which [had] hitherto bound society together by the mutual cohesions and attractions of habits, manners, institutions, morals, and literature." Story found his country in the grip of "a general skepticism—a restless spirit of innovation and change—a fretful desire to provoke discussion of all sorts, under the pretext of free inquiry, or of comprehensive liberalism." This spiritual disease did not simply refuse to hold old things "a matter of reverence or affection"; even worse, it encouraged a "gross over-valuation and inordinate exaggeration of the peculiar advantages and excellencies" of the present age over all others.[5] Story was not against progress—indeed, he firmly embraced the notion of the constant evolution of society—but he agreed with Edmund Burke that "to innovate is not to reform."[6] The skepticism of the age, he thought, was leading mankind to abandon the fundamental truths it had come to know through the course of its history, in favor of blind and often mind-less change.

This spirit of skepticism and innovation had gradually crept to the sur-face and begun to infect the political thinking of the time. By 1832 Story found the political situation in America "truly alarming," and the situa-tion was made worse by the fact that it was accompanied by "no corre-spondent feeling of . . . danger." He expressed his concern vividly to Richard Peters:

> We have been and are too prosperous to be able to rouse ourselves;
> I fear we shall be ruined like all other Republics, and by the same
> means, an overwhelming conceit and confidence in our own wisdom
> and a surrender of our principles at the call of corrupt demagogues.[7]

Story was certain that the "old constitutional doctrines" were not only "fast fading away" but were being replaced by new principles, forged by the new and dangerous public opinion. This new public attitude, he be-lieved, could "augur little good." The infection of this mindless spirit of democracy gnawed at the soul of his beloved republic. The people, upon whom the republic rested (and in whom Story had never had much faith), had become "stupefied . . . by the arts of demagogues and the corrupted influences of party." As a result, the nation had been dragged down into a "state of unexampled distress and suffering" from which it was unlikely to escape.[8]

In 1829 the democratic seeds planted by the Jeffersonian Republicans sprang into full bloom in the form of the grass-roots democracy of Andrew Jackson. The nationalism of Story was never compatible with that of the Jacksonians, and one of the most glaring points of difference between them arose over the efforts to codify the common law. The Codification Movement, which began in the early 1820s, reached maturity in the 1830s. It was a natural corollary of the Jacksonian creed, just as it had been for the Jeffersonians. Both strains of democracy looked with fear on the judicial power, and especially on judicial discretion, and both found comfort in clearly promulgated laws passed by the legislature pursuant to a strictly construed Constitution. The common law was anathema to such political thought. Not only was it a body of "foreign jurisprudence"; it was also seen as nothing more than the arbitrary opinions of judges, which could only undermine constitutional republicanism. It was the Codifica-tion Movement more than anything else that prompted Story to undertake the arduous task of providing exhaustive commentaries on nearly every aspect of American law.[9]

If one must single out one aspect of the common law that most clearly epitomized everything that the proponents of codification found obnoxious, it would have to be equity jurisprudence. "In respect to equity jurisprudence," Story wrote in 1820, "where so much is necessarily left to discretion (...judicial, not to arbitrary discretion), it is of infinite moment that it be administered upon determinate principles."[10] But, in America, there had been considerable deviations from the established principles of equity. Indeed,

> A more broad and undefined discretion has been assumed, and a less stringent obedience to the dictates of authority. Much is left to the habits of thinking of the particular judge, and more to that undefined notion of right and wrong, of hardship and inconvenience, which popular opinions alternately create and justify.[11]

The problem was not that equity lacked exact principles and settled rules but rather that equity had not yet been cultivated as a science. The confusion over equity led to a "spectral dread of it" as being "a transcendental power, acting above the law, and superseding and annulling its operations" at the whim of any judge. Story insisted that equity was, to the contrary, more than any other single department of the law, "completely fenced in by principles." If the common law was to be preserved, it was necessary to cultivate equity as a "science," for, at bottom, equity was the heart of the common law[12] because it "addressed to the consciences of men the beneficent and wholesome principles of justice."[13] Story wrote:

> The principles of equity jurisprudence are of a very enlarged and elevated nature. They are essentially rational, and moulded into a degree of moral perfection which the law has merely aspired to.... The great branches of jurisprudence mutually illustrate and support each other. The principles of one may often be employed with the most captivating felicity in the aid of another; and in proportion as the common law becomes familiar with the lights of equity, its own code will become more useful and more enlightened.[14]

In 1835, after his *Commentaries on Bailments* (1832), his magnificent *Commentaries on the Constitution of the United States* (1833), and his *Commentaries on the Conflict of Laws* (1834) had established his reputation as *the* defender of the common law, Story focused his attention on producing a systematic treatment of equity. The result was the internationally acclaimed *Commentaries on Equity Jurisprudence* (1836), which was followed two years later by an "appropriate sequel," *Commentaries on Equity Pleadings*. It is in these works that Story's equity jurisprudence was comprehensively expressed.

II

Story wrote the commentaries on both equity jurisprudence and equity pleadings with an eye toward educating the students of American law "in the great doctrines of Equity, a subject of almost infinite complexity and variety."[15] He saw the great tradition of equity jurisprudence from Aristotle to Blackstone as having fallen on hard times within America's legal profession. Equity was no longer carefully studied and had never been cultivated as a science. As a result, equity had come to be viewed positively by lawyers and negatively by the codifiers as a source of nearly unbounded judicial discretion. Story's effort was directed toward a regeneration of the original understanding of equity, which had begun with Aristotle: a source of juridical power whereby in particular cases—those in which justice would be lost by too close an adherence to the letter of the law—the positive law could be bent and softened as necessary.

Story did not view his efforts on behalf of equity as entirely original; he thought of them as an American extension of the work Lord Bacon and Lord Hardwicke had begun in England many years before. Bacon's "Ordinances in Chancery," had set the business of chancery on a regular course and, in Story's view, had thereby accomplished for the "practical administration of equity" what his *Novum Organum* had achieved for "the study of physics and experimental philosophy." With procedure in England's chancery thus organized by Bacon, it was left to Lord Hardwicke "to combine the scattered fragments into a scientific system; to define with a broader line the boundaries between the departments of the common law and chancery; and to give certainty and rigor to the principles as well as the jurisdiction of the latter." Story intended to offer no less to his American brethren. He viewed equity as a system of "curious moral machinery" whose principles were at once "enlarged and elevated" yet practical.[16] Equity was that field of the law where the precepts of natural justice were brought down to touch most directly the affairs of men.[17]

Story's equity jurisprudence combined the earlier perspectives of Bacon and Hardwicke on the procedural and substantive aspects of equity and thus can be understood as the last powerful modern articulation of the original Aristotelian concept of juridical equity. Story understood that the efficacy of equity would be better preserved if it came to be viewed as being bound, no less than the common law, to procedure and precedent, the two great principles of the idea of the rule of law. Even though the principles of equity were founded in natural justice or natural law, the jurisdiction of its administration could never be "so wide and extensive as that which arises from the principles of natural justice." In any civilized country—even in Rome—it is necessary to leave "many matters of natural justice wholly unprovided for: from the difficulty of framing any general rules to meet them, and from the doubtful nature of the policy of attempting to give a legal sanction to duties of imperfect obligation, such as charity, gratitude, and kindness."[18] There is, then, a necessary distinction between *natural* equity and *civil* equity.

Civil equity, the more limited concept, is that part of civil law that is distinct from the strict or statutory law. Story accepted (and quoted as his authority) Aristotle's definition of equity as the "correction of the law" whenever the strict law is defective by reason of its universality.[19]

In this sense, as the correction of the strict law, Story understood equity as being necessarily applied to the "interpretation and limitation of the words of positive or written laws; by construing them, not according to the letter but according to the reason and spirit of them."[20] In this method of equitable interpretation, the primary rule was the same as it was for interpretations of common law:

The fundamental maxim . . . in the interpretation of statutes, or positive laws, is, that the intention of the legislature is to be followed. This intention is to be gathered from the words, the context, the subject matter, the effects and consequences, and the spirit and reason are to be ascertained, not from vague conjecture, but from the motives and language apparent on the face of the law.[21]

This procedure of interpreting the law by its equity is necessary in "every rational system of jurisprudence, if not in name, at least in substance." This is the case because "every system of laws must necessarily be defective" and cannot possibly furnish rules applicable to the infinite variety of human affairs. Under any system of positive laws (or "any code, however minute and particular") "cases must occur, to which the antecedent rules cannot be applied without injustice, or to which they cannot be applied at all. It is the office, therefore, of a judge to consider, whether the antecedent rule does apply, or ought, according to the intention of the lawgiver, to apply to a given case."[22]

This emphasis on equitable interpretation, Story remarked, had led to many mistaken notions concerning the powers of courts of equity, and Story believed it necessary to clear the air of these erroneous impressions. First, he insisted, the "proposition that Equity will relieve against a general rule of law is . . . neither sanctioned by principle, nor by authority." He accepted Sir Joseph Jekyll's dictum that

Discretion is a science, not to act arbitrarily, according to men's wills, and private affections; so that discretion, which is executed . . . is to be governed by the rules of law and equity, which are not to oppose, but each in its turn to be subservient to the other. This discretion, in some cases follows the law implicitly; in others assists it, and advances the remedy; in others again it relieves against the abuse, or allays the rigor of it. But, in no case, does it contradict or overturn the grounds or principles thereof. . . .[23]

Second, Story dismissed as "equally untenable" the proposition that every matter that is inconsistent with the intention of the legislator or is contrary to the principles of natural justice should find relief in equity. He observed that,

so far from a Court of Equity supplying universally the defects of positive legislation, or peculiarly carrying into effect the intent, as contradistinguished from the text of the Legislature, it is governed by the same rules of interpretation as a Court of Law; and is often compelled to stop, where the letter of law stops. It is the duty of every court of justice, whether of Law or of Equity, to consult the intention of the Legislature. And in the discharge of this duty, a Court of Equity is not invested with a larger, or more liberal, discretion than a Court of Law.[24]

Third, Story insisted that courts of equity are, contrary to some prevalent opinions, surely bound by precedent; nothing could be more absurd or more dangerous than the assumption that every case in equity "is to be decided upon circumstances according to the arbitration or discretion of the Judge, acting according to his own notions *ex aequo et bono.*" Story chose rather to embrace the opinion of Blackstone, who had held courts of equity to be "a labored connected system, governed by established rules, and bound down by precedents, from which they do not depart."[25] To those who embraced this trilogy of errors concerning the powers of courts of equity, Story offered an emphatic refutation:

If . . . a Court of Equity . . . did possess the unbounded jurisdiction, which has been thus generally ascribed to it, of correcting, controlling, moderating, and even superseding the law, and enforcing all the rights, as well as the charities, arising from natural law and justice, and of freeing itself from all regard to former rules and precedents, it would be the most gigantic in its sway, and the most formidable instrument of arbitrary power, that could well be devised. It would literally place the whole rights and property of the community under the arbitrary will of the Judge, acting, if you please, *arbitrio et bono,* according to his own notions and conscience, but still acting with a despotic and sovereign authority.[26]

In Story's view the most important maxim of equity jurisprudence was *Aequitas Sequitur Legem:* "Equity follows the Law." The jurisdiction of equity, he believed, must, no less than ordinary legal jurisdiction, be of a permanent and fixed character. Equity, like the law, had a definite body of fixed principles upon which courts of equity were to act. And, perhaps most important, equity was a part of the law; it was not some philosophic scheme divorced from the law itself. After he had attempted to dismiss the inaccurate or inadequate notions of equity that had poisoned public opinion toward equity jurisprudence, Story attempted to give some positive statement of equity.

"Equity Jurisprudence" he defined as "that portion of remedial justice which is exclusively administered by a Court of Equity, as contradistinguished from the portion of remedial justice, which is exclusively administered by a Court of Common Law."[27] In light of the fundamental maxim "Equity follows the law," the jurisdiction of courts of equity extends only to the relief a court of law would grant if it could. Whenever a *"complete, certain,* and *adequate* remedy exists at law, Courts of Equity have generally no jurisdiction."[28]

In the courts of law "there are certain prescribed forms of action, to which the party must resort to furnish him a remedy; and, if there be no prescribed form to reach such a case, he is remediless" in the law courts.[29] It is in such cases that equity serves as an "auxiliary to the law."[30] Story elaborated by noting that

There are many cases in which a simple judgment for either party, without qualifications, or conditions, or peculiar arrangements, will not do entire justice *ex aequo et bono* to either party. Some modifications of the rights of both parties may be required; some restraints on one side, or on the other, or perhaps on both sides; some adjustments involving reciprocal obligations or duties; some compensatory or preliminary, or concurrent proceedings to fix control or equalize rights; some qualifications or conditions, present or future, temporary or permanent, to be annexed to the exercise of rights on the redress of injuries.[31]

In such cases, where ordinary courts of law are incapable "from their very character and organization" of giving relief, courts of equity are not so restrained:

Although they have prescribed forms of proceeding, the latter are flexible, and may be suited to the different postures of cases. They may adjust their decrees so as to meet most, if not all, of these exigencies; and they may vary, qualify, restrain, and model the remedy, so as to suit it to mutual and adverse claims, controlling equities, and the real and substantial rights of all the parties.[32]

The great object of equity in its role as auxiliary to the law is justice; and justice often demands more than ordinary courts of law can provide.

Quoting Blackstone's ruminations, Story outlined the more important powers and duties of courts of equity. Such courts are established

> to detect latent frauds and concealments, which the process of Courts of Law is not adapted to reach; to enforce the execution of such matters of trust and confidence as are binding in conscience, though not cognizable in a Court of Law; to deliver from such dangers as are owing to misfortune and oversight; and to give a more specific relief, and more adapted to the circumstances of the case, than can always be obtained by the generality of the rules of the positive or common law.[33]

Thus it is of the greatest importance that remedies at law be plain, adequate, and complete. If they are not, equity will very likely assert a jurisdiction. In order to effect a plain, adequate, and complete remedy in all cases, the jurisdiction of equity courts is sometimes concurrent with the jurisdiction of law courts, sometimes exclusive of it, and sometimes auxiliary to it;[34] but it is never superior to it in any abstract, theoretical sense.

Story, however, did embrace the idea that equity reached to all cases where natural justice gave a right but common law had provided no means of enforcing it. It was not his position, however, that equity, in contradistinction to the common law, had a direct reference to natural law; in his view, equity was a part of the broader common law that itself was a reflection of the natural law and a system of rights and obligations dictated by natural justice. He understood the common law—and thereby the spirit of the common law, equity—as a "system having its foundations in natural reason; but at the same time, built up and perfected by artificial doctrines, adapted and moulded by the artificial structure of society."[35] Equity, like the broader common law, was founded on the law of nature. It was a system of rules that had existed "antecedently" to man and, through history, had been given concrete expression in statutes, treatises, and, especially, in judicial opinions. But it was in no way dependent on these literary devices for its existence. The law of nature, to Story, was "nothing more than those rules which human reason deduces from the various relations of man, to form his character, and regulate his conduct."[36] Many of these rules of human conduct found themselves clearly promulgated in the strict law, while others were left to the realm of equity jurisprudence by their very nature and character. Therefore, equity jurisprudence had a particular and specific jurisdiction, based on the objects left to its cognizance.

Story found the "peculiar province" of equity courts to lie in administering the defects of the strict law "in cases of *frauds, accidents, mistakes,* or *trusts."* In cases of fraud, equity would interfere and would compel complete restitution; in cases of accident or mistake, equity would interfere to administer proper and effectual relief by commanding specific performance; in cases of trusts, equity would apply the principles of conscience and enforce the expressed or implied trusts according to good faith. Basically, Story understood equity as Hamilton had in *The Federalist:* as a means of offering relief from "hard bargains." He further elaborated his understanding of equity thus:

> Sometimes, by fraud or accident, a party has an advantage in proceeding in a court of ordinary jurisdiction, which must necessarily make that court an instrument of injustice, if the suit be suffered; and equity, to prevent such a manifest wrong, will interpose, and restrain the party from using his unfair advantage. Sometimes, one party holds completely at his mercy the rights of another, because there is no witness to the transaction, or it lies in the privity of an adverse interest; equity in such cases will compel a discovery of the facts, and measure substantial justice to all. Sometimes, the administration of justice is obstructed by certain impediments to a fair decision of the case in a court of law; equity, in such cases, as auxiliary to the law, removes the impediments. Sometimes, property is in danger of being lost or injured, pending a litigation; equity there interposes to preserve it. Sometimes oppressive and vexatious suits are wantonly pursued and repeated by litigious parties; for the preservation of peace and of justice, equity imposes in such cases an injunction of forbearance.[37]

It was of grave importance to Story that students of the law be able to distinguish between what we have called the substantive and the procedural aspects of equity jurisprudence. On the one hand, there was the general sense of equity "which is equivalent to universal or natural justice, *ex aequo et bono,"* and, on the other hand, there was the technical sense "which is descriptive of the exercise of jurisdiction over peculiar rights and remedies."[38] Those who confused the two aspects often concluded—incorrectly—that "Courts of Law can never administer justice with reference to principles of universal or natural justice, but are confined to rigid, severe, and uncompromising rules, which admit of no equitable considerations." To the contrary, the decisions in courts of law are often "guided by the most liberal equity." For courts of law to be rigidly bound by the mere letter of the law would be as inefficacious and dangerous as if courts of equity were completely unbound by the letter of the law. Considerations of law and considerations of equity were so closely knitted together that even the question of whether all remedial justice should be in one class of courts or split into two was more often debated than answered. Story concluded that this question could "never ... be susceptible of any universal solution, applicable to all times, and all nations, and all changes in jurisprudence." It would always depend on the "mixed question of public policy and private convenience."[39] Although he was unwilling to make universal proclamations on the question of jurisdictions, Story did have a particular personal view of the matter.

He believed that "the administration of equity should be by a distinct court, having no connection with, or dependence upon, any court of common law." Should both law and equity be administered in the same court, it would be a dangerous judicial arrangement for two reasons. First, the equity of a case might transfer itself to the law of the case and thus give an unwholesome liberality to the decision of the court; second, the questions of law in a particular case might tend to "narrow down the comprehensive liberality of equity." Either circumstance could, and probably would, occur if equity and law were mixed in the same jurisdiction. Such a mixture, "whenever it takes place," Story asserted, "is decidedly bad in flavor and quality."[40]

Story viewed separate jurisdictions as beneficial for several other reasons. Using a "division of labor" argument, he suggested that a steady devotion to one pursuit (either equity or law) would give the jurist greater accuracy and acuteness: "the subdivision of labor gives greater perfection to the whole machinery" of justice. There was also the problem that much of the business of a court of equity consisted in granting injunctions obtained at law; a conflict of interest was quite probable. But the most important reason he found was that separate jurisdictions of law and equity would "act as checks and balances to each other." This rather novel view of a divided judicial authority held that a rigid separation would "have the most salutary influence upon all judicial proceedings" by keeping the courts sufficiently independent so as to "prevent any undue ascendency by either."[41]

Story recognized the inherent danger of lodging law and equity in the same hands, as had Anti-Federalists "Brutus" and the "Federal Farmer" during the struggle for ratification of the Constitution.[42] But Story's view was broader: not only was equity a danger to law, but law was also a danger to equity. Courts of both law and equity were necessary to the administration of justice, and justice was more likely to be realized where equity could not easily slip over and liberalize the strictness of the law and where the law, in turn, could not restrict the more liberal principles of equity. Story realized that, in the states where such jurisdictional questions were being asked, those favoring a union of law and equity in the same jurisdiction would have recourse to the federal analogy. However, to him, the federal analogy was inappropriate. It was at the state level where the "great mass of equity suits" would take place. The federal courts exercised only a limited jurisdiction in equity cases. They could, by "the qualified nature of their authority over persons," take cognizance of suits in equity only "where the United States or aliens, or citizens of other states are parties." Given the fact that the Constitution created a judicial *power* rather than an intricately elaborate judicial *system,* there was an "inherent difficulty in separating the supreme jurisdiction at law from that in equity."[43] Thus, Story had no difficulty in accepting as legitimate the rigid procedural distinction between law and equity that Congress had imposed on the inferior federal courts in the Judiciary and Process Acts of the first Congress.

He recognized that there was a close connection between substantive equity and procedural equity, between the idea itself, *ex aequo et bono,* and the administration of that idea. In particular, he found that the lack of knowledge of special equity pleadings had contributed in no small way to the general loss of respect for equity jurisprudence. To remedy this state of affairs, he turned his attention from the principles of equity to the forms of equity. In this sense, his *Commentaries on Equity Jurisprudence* and his *Commentaries on Equity Pleadings* form a comprehensive whole.

Joseph Story considered his *Commentaries on Equity Pleadings* an "appropriate sequel" to his earlier work on equity jurisprudence. In the later work, on pleadings, his intention was to connect the principles of equity he had developed in his work on equity jurisprudence with "the forms of the proceedings, by which rights are vindicated and wrongs are redressed, in Courts of Equity."[44] In American law, Story saw a "looseness and inartificial structure" in its pleadings. This betrayed "an imperfect knowledge both of the principles and forms," which in turn not only deprived the pleadings in the American legal process of "elegance and symmetry" but also subjected them "to the coarser imputation of slovenliness." But a lack of elegance and polish was not the only problem. The general lack of emphasis on special pleadings had resulted in a superficiality in American legal education.[45]

"The forms of pleading," argued Story, "are not, as some may rashly suppose, mere trivial forms; they not unfrequently involve the essence of the defence; and the discipline, which is acquired by a minute attention to their structure, is so far from being lost labor, that it probably more than all other employments, leads the student to close and symmetrical logic." Special pleading, in Story's opinion, contained the "quintessence of the law."[46] This attention to detail helped to develop a "scrutinizing logic" that would counteract any tendency to "undue speculation." By encouraging an uncompromising attention to the forms of the ancient law, equity pleadings led the way to a deeper understanding of the substance of equity by submerging the student in the deep currents of the common law itself.

It was not only necessary that the principles of equity be scientifically cultivated to insure its uniformity and certainty; it was also essential that forms should be prescribed for its administration. This was of special significance in the federal courts, where procedure alone separated law from equity. In a very fundamental sense, the preservation of the substantive principles of equity depended on the procedural forms of equity pleadings, for only by reducing both form and substance to clearly exposited principles and rules could equity be presented as safe and thus be secured against the growing democratic wave of the Codification Movement.

Story's purpose in writing his massive commentaries on many parts of the common law, including his *Commentaries on Equity Jurisprudence* and *Commentaries on Equity Pleadings,* was to commend and recommend the common law "upon true, old, and elevated principles"[47] and, while adamantly denying the methodology of the Codification Movement, to introduce uniform principles and rules of law and equity throughout the nation, at both the state and federal level. Story firmly believed that it was necessary to "have sufficient knowledge of the old law" and yet not be "a slave to its forms." Equity, like the common law generally, was not a static entity but a dynamic system of jurisprudence made up of "artificial doctrines" but resting firmly on the foundation of the law of nature. It was natural and totally acceptable to Story that, as society progressed from its rude beginnings, both law and equity should be invigorated "with new principles, not from the desire of innovation, but the love of improvement."[48] It was the growing popularity of radical innovation that he feared the most. Against this ominous threat, Story attempted to rally the thoughtful men of his profession. "I would speak," he said,

> to the consciences of honorable men, and ask how they can venture, without any knowledge of existing laws, to recommend changes which may cut deep into the quick of remedial justice, or bring into peril all that is valuable in jurisprudence by its certainty, its policy, or its antiquity. Surely they need not be told, how slow every good system of laws must be in consolidating; and how easily the rashness of an hour may destroy what ages have scarcely cemented in a solid form. The oak, which requires centuries to rear its trunk, and stretch its branches, and strengthen its fibres, and fix its roots, may yet be levelled in an hour. It may breast the tempest of a hundred years, and survive the scathing of the lightning. It may even acquire vigor from

its struggles with the elements, and strike its roots deeper and wider as it rises in its majesty; and yet a child, in the very wantonness of folly, may in an instant destroy it by removing a girdle of its bark.[49]

III

Story sought a cure for the political distemper of his age in the common law. He was not opposed to *any* codification (he even thought the common law could be strengthened by *some* codification);[50] what he opposed was the immoderation of most of the codifiers. His view of man was less confident than theirs. To suppose that man is capable of framing a comprehensive legal code, he argued, "is to suppose that he is omniscient, all-wise, and all-powerful; that he is perfect, or that he can attain perfection; that he can see all the future in the past; and that the past is present to him in all its relations." Such an assumption struck Story as preposterous: "The statement of such a proposition carries with it its own refutation. While man remains as he is, his powers and capacities, and acts, must forever be imperfect."[51]

Story understood law to be something broader and deeper than mere positive decrees of the public will. "Laws," he insisted, "are the very soul of a people; not merely those which are contained in the letter of their ordinances and statute books, but still more those which have grown up of themselves from their manners, and religion and history."[52] Law, to Story, was "founded, not upon any will, but on the discovery of a right already existing, which is to be drawn either from the internal legislation of human reason, or the historical development of the nation."[53] Hence, mere popular consent was not, for him, the true law; the common law was the true law. The common law drew its authority not from the transient decrees of a legislative body but from both philosophy and history; it was the point where theory and practice in human affairs touched. And the relationship between law and society was symbiotic: not only was law formed by the manners, morals, and habits of a people, but it in turn operated forcibly and silently to help form people's manners, morals, and habits.

The main thrust of the Codification Movement was aimed at reducing the uncertainty of the common law, which the codifiers saw as its great flaw. Their intention was to replace it with clear and objective codes that would not need judicial discretion to be interpreted and administered. But the uncertainty attributed to the common law by "the vulgar," Story argued, was not the result of judicial discretion but rather resulted naturally from the "endless complexity and variety of human actions."[54] Immeasurable uncertainties of this kind could not be resolved by any legal code but only by human judgment that took into account not only the particular circumstances of each case but also the ancient laws, "fashioned from age to age by wise and learned judges."[55] This ancient or common law was composed of general principles, accepted not simply because they were old but because they contained certain truths to which man could look for direction and guidance. To Story, the abandonment of the common law in favor of "comprehensive" codes would only introduce more uncertainty, in the form of judicial discretion, into the legal process.[56]

Another advantage Story saw in the common law was its tendency to be less static than statute law. Although the common law was a system of "general juridical truths," it was still capable of "continually expanding with the progress of society." In this the common law "resembles the natural sciences where new discoveries continually lead the way to new and sometimes astonishing results."[57] Indeed, the common law itself was a science. There is no science, Story wrote,

> so vast, so intricate, and so comprehensive, as that of jurisprudence. In the widest extent it may be said almost to compass every human action; and in its minute details, to measure every human duty. If we contemplate it in the highest order of subjects which it embraces, it can scarcely be surpassed in dignity. It searches into and expounds the elements of morals and ethics, and the eternal law of nature, illustrated and supported by the eternal law of revelation.[58]

Story accepted as his obligation the "scientific" exposition of the common law in order to brace it against the passionate gusts of the codifiers. His "science," however, following in the tradition of Blackstone and Kent, was an attempt to distinguish and clarify parts of the common law by offering a "clear exposition of principles and authorities" that had been scattered in a huge mass of reports and treatises.[59] This "science" was an attempt to organize and methodize the grand principles of the common law and thereby reduce the obscurity and strengthen the tradition of the common law in America. True to the tradition to which he subscribed, he adopted the mode of writing commentaries on points of law that braided together legal treatises, political philosophy, and judicial opinions into a cord with which to tie the past to the present in order the better to prepare for the future.

Story's major premise was always that the common law offered a safer course for republican government than did the utopian solutions of the codifiers. Although the common law was mutable and flexible, it was not arbitrary. To be sure, *judicial* discretion was not the same as discretion.[60] The common law, he insisted, "controls the arbitrary discretion of judges, and puts the case beyond the peculiar opinions and complexional reasoning of a particular judge; for he is hemmed around by authority on every side." Of no slight weight in moderating judicial opinions was the "consciousness that the decision will form a permanent precedent, affecting all future cases." This knowledge would necessarily introduce "great caution and deliberation" in giving an opinion. Story saw common-law interpretations as pointing "to one great object—certainty and uniformity of interpretation,"[61] and, to preserve that certainty and uniformity in the administration of justice, it was necessary to preserve the common law.

Story's equity jurisprudence, like his common-law jurisprudence generally, was intended to preserve as much of the older natural-law tradition as possible in the face of growing professional and popular distrust of that tradition and to combat the growing trust in legal positivism.

Story was, in sum, the last major defender of the original understanding of equity as transmitted from Aristotle to Blackstone. He saw equity not as a mere set of procedural remedies but as a system of jurisprudence, an auxiliary to the strict law, which aimed at an understanding of justice that transcended the fluctuating decrees of popular consent. More than any other man of his time, Story sought to recover and preserve the ethical and moral basis of the law. He attempted this recovery and preservation through the scientific elaboration of the vast tradition of the common law, of which equity was a part.

Story's series of commentaries offered an alternative to drastic codification. Through his herculean efforts, his beloved common law was given greater uniformity and clarity. Legal commentary, combined with limited codification, could, in his view, "bring the law into a state approximating the exactness of Science." By his voluminous outpouring, he was able to undermine the movement of the most zealous Benthamites toward a complete codification of the common law, but, though he was able to slow and even to weaken the Codification Movement, he was unable to stop its march for very long.

Through his *Commentaries on Equity Jurisprudence* and his *Commentaries on Equity Pleadings,* Joseph Story made a valiant effort to teach both his profession and the public a lesson in the law: that equity is a substantive body of law, necessary to the administration of justice, which can be abused or even destroyed by disregard for its procedure. This lesson either fell on deaf ears or was misunderstood. In 1848, only three years after Story's death, the Codification Movement won its first major victory in New York, with the adoption of the Field Code of Civil Procedure. With this victory began the transformation of the substantive idea of equity through reform of its procedure.

Five Procedure over Substance: The Codification Movement and the Transformation of American Equity

I n the history of the Codification Movement in America, no figure looms larger than David Dudley Field of New York. Field provided the movement with its theoretical framework in much the same way Joseph Story had provided the theoretical framework for the defense of the common law. What is striking is that Field was motivated by the same understanding of the law that had motivated Story. Like Story, he believed the common law to be founded on natural justice, which in turn rested on the Puritan foundation of his own Christian faith.[1]

I

David Dudley Field, brother of Stephen J. Field, associate justice of the United States Supreme Court, articulated a jurisprudence that fell between Jeremy Bentham's and Joseph Story's. He differed from Bentham, the theoretical father of codification, because he was "concerned centrally with the improvement of legal administration and not with the reform of society as a whole"; he differed from Story because, "although not interested in codifying law down to the last detail, he did propose to operate over the whole field of law, both substantive and remedial."[2] Like Story and unlike Bentham, Field was a lawyer and not a detached critic of the common law.

Field entered the legal profession in 1830, at the age of twenty-five, "with a feeling of reverence amounting almost to awe." He had immersed himself in the traditional study of law to such an extent that he could later boast that if there was anything which he understood "it was the practice at common law and in equity as then established in the Court of New York."[3] Thus, he began his assault on the common law as an insider, one who held the law in great esteem. He advocated codification of the law not to destroy the common law "but to preserve it by eliminating its defects and rendering it into language understandable to the people as well as the Bench and Bar." His approach was basically the historical approach that Joseph Story had adopted; but whereas Story had been satisfied to restate existing law and demonstrate to the present the relevance of the past, Field went further. He ultimately sought not only to restate the existing law but also to cut off its "excrescences" and to amend it "to meet modern conditions."[4]

The seed of Field's understanding of legal reform was the view that all positive law should be founded on natural justice and that positive law should be stated in clear and concise language, "intelligible to lawyer and layman alike," and he planned to go "far beyond anything that had already been done to reform the basic structure of both substantive and procedural law."[5] The deepest split between Story's jurisprudence and Field's was over the relationship between the substance of the law and the law's procedure. For Story, procedure—especially the ancient procedure of the common law—served to illustrate and elevate the substance of the law; for Field, it simply undermined it. Story understood the rigid separation of equity procedure from legal procedure as necessary to the achievement of substantive justice; Field, on the other hand, saw the union of law and equity as "the subordination in all things of form to substance."[6] What Story saw as necessary to justice, Field saw as destructive of it.

Field believed that justice could be served only if the dead legal underbrush of ages past could be cleared from its path. An attention to procedure was essential to substantive justice, but that procedure had to be clear, concise, and simple. He was persuaded "that a radical reform of legal procedure in all its departments [was] demanded by the interests of justice and by the voice of the people; that a uniform course of proceeding in all cases legal and equitable [was] entirely practicable and ... expedient; and that a radical reform should aim at such uniformity, and at the abolition of all useless forms and proceedings."[7] Thus, though Field's objective was to reform civil procedure by merging law and equity proceedings into one simplified procedure, what he intended was only an administrative blending of procedure, and for him this did not imply an abolition of the "inherent distinctions"[8] between law and equity.

Field's active efforts on behalf of procedural reform in New York began in 1837. He carried on a letter-writing campaign to the state legislature, appeared before a legislative committee to offer testimony on the need for reform, ran for the state legislature himself, and even drafted bills to be introduced in the legislature by a colleague whose success in politics had been greater than his own.[9] In 1845 the legislature called for a constitutional convention to meet the next year. Because of his radical views on procedural reform, Field was denied the opportunity to sit as a delegate in the convention, but he carried on a regular correspondence with the delegates and maintained a heavy newspaper campaign, including a series of articles, titled "The Reorganization of the Judiciary," that appeared in the New York *Evening Post* in 1848.[10]

The new state constitution, which went into effect on January 1, 1847, contained specific provisions for the reform of procedural law. Field, anticipating that legislative action would follow upon these provisions, published a short pamphlet called *What Shall be Done With the Practice of the Courts?*[11] This was followed by a memorial to the state legislature advocating a "radical reform of legal procedure" and signed by "sixty-one distinguished members of the Bar of New York."[12]

In April, 1847, the New York legislature established the State Commission on Pleading and Practice to propose revisions of the civil procedure. Field, although nominated for membership on this commission, was rejected for being too extreme. However, after one of the original members of the committee resigned, Field was finally appointed, on September 29, 1847, by a joint resolution of the legislature.[13] Between April and September, 1847, he had produced yet another polemic: *Some Suggestions Respecting the Rules to be Established by the Supreme Court*.[14] In February, 1848, the commission presented to the legislature its first report, which contained a draft of an *Act to Simplify and Abridge the Practice and Pleadings and Proceedings of the Courts of the State*. After some amendment, this draft was enacted into law on April 12, 1848.[15] The law went into effect on July 1, 1848. It was written in the form of a code with 391 "brief, gnomic, Napoleonic sections, tightly worded and skeletal," and was called the "Code of Procedure" or, more commonly, the "Field Code."[16]

The crux of the Field Code was contained in its sixty-second section, which declared:

> The distinction between actions at law and suits in equity, and the forms of all such actions and suits heretofore existing, are abolished; and there shall be in this state, hereafter, but one form of action, for the enforcement or protection of private rights and the redress or prevention of private wrongs, which shall be denominated a civil action.[17]

Thus, the Code of Civil Procedure "abolished common law forms and merged law and equity in greatly simplified procedure." One commentator was led to remark: "The science of special pleading, and the learning therein which the most eminent professors have acquired by long years of laborious study, are swept away as 'needless distinctions, scholastic subtleties and dead forms which have disfigured and encumbered our jurisprudence.'"[18]

A remarkable fact is that, while the Field Code started a general conflagration that spread rapidly through the other states, it was nearly snuffed out in New York itself. Reenacted and amended several times by 1880, its once skeletal form (391 sections) sagged under the weight of 3,356 sections. Field himself came to regard it as a "monstrosity."[19] Without waiting to witness the effects of the Field Code in New York, the other states zealously joined in the codification effort.[20]

II

In 1849 Judge Robert Wells of Missouri sounded the call to assemble behind Field when he drafted a measure for reform that, like the Field Code, abolished the procedural distinction between law and equity.[21] Massachusetts followed suit in 1850 with a modified version of procedural reform. Under the direction of future United States Supreme Court Justice Benjamin R. Curtis, the Massachusetts Commission modified the state practice of special pleadings but seems never to have contemplated the complete merger of common law and equitable remedies.[22] In 1851 California adopted a version of the Field Code, and, by the outbreak of the Civil War, Iowa, Minnesota, Indiana, Ohio, the Washington Territory, Nebraska, Wisconsin, and Kansas had followed suit by reforming their civil procedures.[23] In 1861 Nevada adoped the Field Code, and by the end of the century so had the Dakotas, Idaho, Arizona, Montana, the Carolinas, Wyoming, Utah, Colorado, Oklahoma, and New Mexico.[24]

The widespread adoption of the Field Code by so many other states did not occur without criticism. The most common declamation was against the attempt of one state to adopt the code of procedure of another. This view, most forcefully articulated by Dean Henry Ingersoll of the University of Tennessee, was not so much a theoretical attack against codification generally as an attack against adopting a "foreign" code; in particular, it was an assault against the adopting of procedural codes of commercial states by noncommercial states. Ingersoll thundered:

During . . . Reconstruction . . . the legal practice of the State [of North Carolina] was reconstructed by the adoption of the New York Code of Civil Procedure, with all its penalties and high-pressure machinery adapted to the conditions of an alert, eager, pushing commercial community. Rip Van Winkle was not more surprised on returning to his native village after his long sleep than were the lawyers of the old "Tar Heel State." . . . This new fangled commercial machine . . . was as well adapted to their condition as were the light driving buggies of the Riverside Park to the rough roads of the Black mountains, or the garb of the Broadway dandy to the turpentine stiller. . . . North Carolina had about as much use for the system as she had for a clearing house, a Central Park, or a Stock Exchange.[25]

There was also a lingering tendency among conservative lawyers throughout the country to regard all codification efforts as nothing but "love of innovation" and a most glaring example of "barbaric empiricism."[26] The last stronghold of the old order was—not surprisingly—the Supreme Court of the United States.

III

Before the adoption of the Field Code the effects of state codification on the procedure of the federal courts were slight because the acts of Congress governing federal procedure had always tended to "prescribe for the federal courts in a state the rules of practice of the courts of that state . . . as of some prescribed date, such as the date of admission to the union." In 1842 an act of Congress authorizing the Supreme Court to promulgate federal rules of equity also gave it the power to promulgate uniform rules in regard to practice at common law. The Supreme Court took no action, preferring, it appears, to let procedure differ among the districts.

When codification in the form of the New York Code of 1848 reached the drastic point of merging law and equity, confusion and dissent mushroomed. It became so great that in 1872 Congress passed the Conformity Act,[27] which required practice in the federal courts to conform with that of the states in which the courts were held. But the Supreme Court resisted mightily the merger of law and equity.

In general, the Supreme Court continued to embrace Joseph Story's understanding of law and equity.[28] Thus, in 1851, Chief Justice Taney, writing the opinion in *Bennett* v. *Butterworth,* insisted that, on the federal level, the distinction between law and equity was not a matter of legislative fiat or judicial rule-making but was established by the Constitution. Law and equity could not be merged in federal judicial process. In 1857, in a dissenting opinion in an admiralty case, *Dupont* v. *Vance,* Justice John Campbell invoked the words of James Kent in defense of the "traditional accoutrements of the common law":

I entertain a decided opinion that the established principles of pleading, which compose what is called the science, are national, concise,
luminious, and admirably adapted to the investigation of truth, and
ought, consequently, to be very cautiously touched by the hand of
innovation.[29]

In 1858 the Court again came to the defense of common-law procedure.
Speaking for a unanimous Court in *McFaul* v. *Ramsey,* Justice Robert
Grier reiterated the theoretical relationship Story had elaborated in his
equity commentaries:

This system, matured by the wisdom of ages, founded upon principles
of truth and sound reason, has been ruthlessly abolished in many of
our States, who have rashly substituted in its place the suggestions of
sociologists, who invest new codes and systems of pleading to order.
But this attempt to abolish all species, and establish a single genus, is
found to be beyond the power of legislative omnipotence. They cannot
compel the human mind not to distinguish between things that differ.
The distinction between the different forms of actions for different
wrongs, requiring different remedies, lies in the nature of things; it is
absolutely inseparable from the correct administration of justice in
common law courts. [At 525]

However profound these views, the Supreme Court was fighting a losing
battle to preserve the rituals of the common law.[30] As the Codification
Movement swept through the states, legal education came to reflect its
tenets. In code states, the younger lawyers naturally came to know code
pleading rather than common-law pleading. When it came time for judicial
appointments to the federal bench, the new district judges carried with
them their easy familiarity with code pleadings. Eventually some of these
code-state judges would be appointed to the Supreme Court of the United
States. The first group of them arrived in the 1860s: Noah Swayne from
Ohio, Samuel F. Miller from Iowa, and Stephen J. Field from California.
In a clear display of the political nature of the Court, the old guards of the
common law were gradually replaced by the young vanguard of codifiers.
Even the nation's highest tribunal proves ultimately to be a representative
body.

IV

Around the turn of the century the American Bar Association concluded
that "legislative control of practice was demonstrably inefficient, and that
the conformity act had produced no real conformity between state and
federal practice." In seeking a remedy for this situation the Association
backed a bill in Congress that would provide that the power to promulgate

federal rules of procedure be turned over to the United States Supreme Court.[31] This movement was met by a small but solid wall of Senate disapproval. For twenty years the opposition succeeded in blocking the act. Between 1925 and 1933 it was led by Senator Walsh of Montana, a member of the Senate Judiciary Committee. In 1933, however, Walsh died, and opposition to the bill was interred with him. In June, 1934, the promulgation bill was finally passed. Its provisions were quite new:

> Be it enacted . . . that the Supreme Court of the United States shall have the power to prescribe, by general rules, for the district courts of the United States and for the courts of the District of Columbia, the forms of process, writs, pleadings, and motions, and the practice and procedure in civil actions at law.[32]

Although the Supreme Court had possessed the rule-making power with regard to equity procedure since the Process Acts, it now had that power for all civil actions. If this was not startling enough, the legislature went even farther:

> SEC. 2. The court may at any time unite the general rules prescribed by it for cases in equity with more in actions at law as to secure one form of civil action and procedure for both. . . .[33]

Thus, after nearly a century, the Field Code's central provision—the obliteration of the procedural distinction between law and equity—had found its way into the federal judiciary.

The Court did not immediately move to effect the merger, however. On June 3, 1935, it appointed an advisory committee to draft rules and submit further proposals for the Court's consideration.[34] During this period both the bench and the bar were active and influential in drafting rules. This fact no doubt served to forestall opposition and to soften criticism from the legal profession and render it "friendly to the system when it went into operation."[35] In 1938 the Court formally adopted one system of civil procedure, merging proceedings at law with proceedings at equity, and promulgated the new Rules of Civil Procedure.[36]

V

The Supreme Court's rule-making power in equity proceedings, granted by the Process Acts, had always reflected the original assumption of Chief Justice John Jay, in 1792, that such procedure would be guided by the great tradition of equity jurisprudence as developed in the English Court of Chancery. The Court's first set of equity rules was promulgated in 1822 and contained thirty-three rules.[37] The second set—ninety-two in number—was created in 1842.[38] And, in 1912, the Court produced a comprehensive reform of the equity rules, positing eighty-one new rules of equity procedure.[39] Prior to 1938 the Court made only three amendments to the rules promulgated in 1912. Throughout its history the Court had exercised its equity rule-making with an eye to the necessity of maintaining a rigid procedural distinction between law and equity. Such a distinction was seen as necessary to republican safety.

The main bodies of equity rules—those of 1822, 1842, and 1912—were extremely detailed. They outlined in clear language the exact procedure to be followed, from the filing of the bill to the taking of testimony and the keeping of records. The emphasis on such detail was necessary to maintain the procedural distinction between the equity jurisdiction and the law jurisdiction of the federal courts.

In 1937 that distinction between equity procedures and law procedures was abolished. On December 20, 1937, Chief Justice Charles Evans Hughes transmitted to Congress the new Rules of Civil Procedure his Court had fashioned pursuant to the Act of 1934. He was requested to add to his letter of transmittal "that Mr. Justice Brandeis does not approve of the adoption of the rules."[40]

In retrospect it would seem that in adopting the Rules of Civil Procedure of 1938 the Court swept away the wisdom that had guided its earlier rule-making. By combining procedures in law with procedures in equity the Court in effect ignored the dangers of equity the Founders had recognized. With the Rules of Civil Procedure of 1938 the Court made it convenient for judges to switch from their shoes of law to their shoes of equity whenever they found the law too restrictive, as the "Federal Farmer," in 1788, had warned that they could.[41] In the attempt to reduce equity to a safe and more certain code, the Court paved the way for the power of equity to be exercised with a disregard for precedent and procedure. By tearing equity loose from the bindings of common-law procedure, it had rendered suits at equity simpler in process but at the price of emasculating equity as a source of substantive law. Equity became nothing more than a set of procedural remedies reflective of the current opinion of a judge. Equity jurisprudence, wrenched free of the common law, was thus deprived of the moderating force of history.

Ironically, as the codifiers moved toward what they perceived as objectivity and certainty in the law, and the concomitant reduction of judicial discretion in the administration of justice, they in fact enhanced subjectivity, uncertainty, and the unfettered judicial discretion so feared by those who had created the Republic.

In 1955 this enhanced subjectivity and uncertainty in the administration of equity reached its peak. That year the Supreme Court handed down the second *Brown* v. *Board of Education of Topeka, Kansas* decision, a decree in equity to implement the constitutional principles it had discovered the year before in the first *Brown* case. In that implementation decision the Court promulgated a new "sociological" understanding of equitable relief—an understanding that had no support in either precedent or principle.

3

The Constitution and the
New Equity

Andrew Jackson   Distinctions in society will always exist under every just
government. Equality of talents, of education, or of
wealth cannot be produced by human institutions. In the
full enjoyment of the gifts of heaven and the fruits of
superior industry, economy, and virtue, every man is
equally entitled to protection by the law.

Six The Emergence of Sociological Equity: The School Desegregation Cases

The school desegregation cases posited a new understanding of equitable relief, and this is one of their most important but least-discussed aspects. In the second historic *Brown* v. *Board of Education of Topeka, Kansas* case (1955) the Supreme Court, in essence, fused the idea of equity to the newly discovered right of psychological equal protection that had been pronounced in *Brown* (I) and, in doing so, generated a new "sociological" understanding of equitable relief. This broadened concept of equity has been a major source of an assumed judicial power to formulate—rather than merely negate—public policies.

Each of the several cases brought and consolidated under the rubric of *Brown*[1] began as a suit to enjoin the enforcement of state laws that either permitted or required separation of the races in the public schools. The cases were united in their appellants' allegation that such separation constituted a violation of the equal protection of the laws guaranteed by the Fourteenth Amendment, but they were separated by "different facts and different local conditions" (*Brown* [I], at 486). The Court, by joining the four cases, denied a fundamental maxim of equity jurisprudence (the opinion of the Chief Justice notwithstanding) by blurring the importance of the distinctiveness of each case.[2] By ignoring the particularity of each case, the Court could confine its attention to what it saw as the unifying "legal question" all of the cases shared: the meaning of

97

equal protection of the laws and, accordingly, the meaning of equality under the Constitution.

The Court's opinion began with a review of its research into the original intention of the Fourteenth Amendment. The Chief Justice pointed out that the evidence concerning the adoption of the amendment was "at best" inconclusive.[3] He then denied the relevance of "tangible factors" in determining whether the doctrine of "separate but equal" was a deprivation of equal protection of the laws. This denial was rhetorically essential because the lower federal court in the Kansas case had "denied relief on the ground that the Negro and white schools were substantially equal with respect to buildings, transportation, curricula, and educational qualifications of teachers."[4] Thus, inequality could not always be proved on the level of tangible evidence.

With the relevance of the concrete factors safely dismissed, Warren then moved into the realm of the intangible. Applauding the social-science *obiter dicta* of the lower court in the Kansas case (in spite of which the lower court had denied relief), he boldly proclaimed that to separate children "solely because of their race generated a *feeling* of inferiority as to their status in the community that *may* affect their hearts and minds in a way *unlikely* ever to be undone" (at 494; italics added). Thus, in the realm of the intangible factors of segregation, it appears that the injury to the complainants was in no way clear, nor was it certain that the injury was irreparable. But, historically, both clarity and irreparable injury were essential for determining whether a court of equity could exert its "extraordinary powers."[5]

It was impossible for the Court to find that the doctrine of "separate but equal" was injurious on the tangible level of politics and policy. It was simply not proved that separate schools could not be equal schools. It was only on the intangible level of "psychological knowledge" and sociological inference that separate schools could become "inherently unequal" (at 494–95).[6] The implications for remedial adjudication were striking. The injury assumed to have been inflicted upon the complainants was to be measured by only one aspect of their situation—their race. Hence all black children everywhere, whenever segregated, were to be considered injured regardless of the quality of the physical facilities of their respective school districts, regardless of their individual perceptions of the alleged deprivation, and regardless even of their academic accomplishments. The conclusion of *Brown* (I) was inescapable: all blacks, solely on the basis of their race, had suffered alike, whether they knew it or not. The individual plaintiff in these equity proceedings had been replaced by an aggrieved social class—a class based solely on what James Madison had called a "frivolous and fanciful distinction."[7]

Chief Justice Warren was not insensitive to the "problems of considerable complexity" the Court would have to face in formulating "appropriate relief" (at 494). To aid the Court in this task, he set a date for reargument so that the Court could enjoy the "full assistance of the parties in formulating decrees" (at 495). The Court asked that the parties, as well as *amici curiae,* address their arguments for the rehearing to a number of questions, among them the following two.

4. Assuming it is decided that segregation in public schools violates the Fourteenth Amendment,

(a) Would a decree necessarily follow providing that, within limits set by normal geographic school districting, Negro children should forthwith be admitted to schools of their choice, or

(b) May this Court, in the exercise of its equity powers, permit an effective gradual adjustment to be brought about from existing segregated systems to a system not based on color distinctions?

5. On the assumption on which questions 4(a) and (b) are based, and assuming further that this Court will exercise its equity powers to the end described in question 4(b),

(a) Should this Court formulate detailed decrees in these cases;

(b) If so, what specific issues should the decrees reach;

(c) Should this Court appoint a special master to hear evidence with a view to recommending specific terms for such decrees;

(d) Should this Court remand to the courts of first instance with directions to frame decrees in these cases, and if so what general directions should the decrees of this Court include and what procedures should the courts of the first instance follow in arriving at the specific terms of more detailed decrees? [At 495, note 13]

The questions presented seem by their nature to imply that the Court was aware of the new course it was preparing to chart across the field of equity jurisprudence. They also seem to reveal the Court's doubt in its own "sound discretion." But the sound discretion of the Court had always been considered the only means of determining whether a federal court should give or deny equitable relief.[8]

I

The reargument on the question of relief ordered in the first *Brown* decision took place April 11–14, 1955. The second *Brown* decision—the implementation decision—was handed down on May 31, 1955. Again, Mr. Chief Justice Warren delivered the opinion of a unanimous Court.

He began by reiterating the "fundamental principle" declared in the first *Brown* opinion, that "racial discrimination in public education is unconstitutional." By inference it was necessary that all "provisions of federal, state, or local law requiring or permitting such discrimination must yield" to the newly discovered "fundamental principle." But merely making existing laws yield was not all that the Court had in mind. It required the implementation—fully and in good faith—of the "governing constitutional principles" (*Brown* II, at 298). At stake, the Chief Justice argued, was the "personal interest of the plaintiffs in admission to public schools as soon as practicable on a nondiscriminatory basis." But, of course, the decree went beyond the merely personal interests of the complainants. *Brown* (I) had elevated the presumed interest of the social class—a "discrete and insular minority"—above the real interest of the individual. Therefore the relief was not to be applicable to the plaintiffs alone, or even to all those "similarly situated" who also felt deprived; it was to extend to all blacks regardless of their particular social, economic, or educational situations. This was a class action, with class relief being awarded that was unique. The relief, the Court determined, would best be decreed by the local federal courts because of their "proximity to local conditions" (at 299) and by exercising their powers of equity. The Chief Justice told why:

> In fashioning and effectuating the decrees, the courts will be guided by equitable principles. Traditionally, equity has been characterized by a practical flexibility in shaping its remedies and by a facility for adjusting and reconciling public and private needs. These cases call for the exercise of these traditional attributes of equity power.

And, he continued:

> To effectuate [the personal interest of the plaintiffs] may call for the elimination of a variety of obstacles in making the transition to school systems operated in accordance with the constitutional principles set forth in [*Brown* (I)]. Courts of equity may properly take into account the public interest in the elimination of such obstacles in a systematic and effective manner. But it should go without saying that the vitality of these constitutional principles cannot be allowed to yield simply because of disagreement with them. [At 300]

Warren's invocation of the federal equity power is curious for two reasons. First, he cited as his precedents cases that had no direct bearing on the issue before him, while other cases, more directly applicable, such as *Truax* v. *Raich* and *Hague* v. *C.I.O.*, were ignored; second, though he spoke of the "traditional attributes" and guiding "principles" of equity as being controlling, he ignored most of the more substantial equitable principles in writing his decree.

II

Warren chose as his precedents two cases of doubtful applicability, *Alexander* v. *Hillman* and *Hecht Co.* v. *Bowles*. *Alexander*, involving a suit for receivership in the dissolution of a corporation, raised the issue of fraudulent trust claims. The passage that caught Warren's attention bears repeating. Mr. Justice Butler had written:

> Treating their established forms as flexible, courts of equity may suit proceedings and remedies to the circumstances of cases and formulate them appropriately to safeguard, conveniently to adjudge, and promptly to enforce substantial rights of all the parties before them. [At 239]

Hecht was a suit for a "statutory injunction" by an administrative agency to enforce the Emergency Price Control Act. The part of that opinion that Chief Justice Warren brought to his support in *Brown* (II) was as follows:

> The historic injunctive process was designed to deter, not to punish. The essence of equity jurisdiction has been the power of the Chancellor to do equity and to mould each decree to the necessities of the particular case. Flexibility rather than rigidity had distinguished it. The qualities of mercy and practicality have made equity the instrument for nice adjustment and reconciliation between the public interest and private needs as well as between competing private claims. [At 329–30]

The most obvious difference between *Alexander* v. *Hillman* and *Hecht* v. *Bowles*, on the one hand, and *Brown* v. *The Board of Education*, on the other, is that the former two, employed as precedents in *Brown*, have a primary and definite relation to property, which is easily susceptible of valuation and more appropriate for an affirmative equitable remedy beyond merely an injunction. Another major point of difference is that, while both *Alexander* and *Hecht* stressed the inherent flexibility of equity (a characteristic recognized and applauded from Aristotle on), they also stressed the importance of bringing the power of equity to address specifically the "necessities" and "circumstances" of the "particular case" (*Alexander* at 239, 242; *Hecht* at 329).

Of the two precedents invoked by Warren in the *Brown* implementation decision, the *Hecht* case is actually the more important. The suit in *Hecht* demanded the "reconciliation between the public interest and private needs" of the parties in the suit. But, unlike *Brown*, the public interest in *Hecht* was represented in a clearly promulgated congressional enactment, the Emergency Price Control Act. The public interest of which Mr. Justice Douglas spoke was not an "abstract principle of justice" seeking vindication in a suit in equity[9] or an imperfect obligation resting only on "conscience and moral duty."[10] It was, on the contrary, the concrete expression of the public will as expressed in a law legitimately formed by the popularly elected representatives of the people. The complainant could offer "tangible" evidence of injury—a monetary loss; the case was not predicated on a mere "feeling" of injury.

The "public interest" doctrine in the *Hecht* case was the direct descendant of the traditional understanding, the general thrust of which was judicial restraint. For, in his opinion in *Hecht,* Mr. Justice Douglas cited as precedent for the "public interest" doctrine a 1943 opinion written by Mr. Justice Stone in *Meredith* v. *Winter Haven.*[11] There Stone had written:

> An appeal to the equity jurisdiction conferred on federal district courts is an appeal to the sound discretion which guides the determinations of courts of equity. Exercise of that discretion by those, as well as by other courts having equity powers, may require them to withhold their relief in furtherance of a *recognized, defined,* public policy. [At 235; italics added]

Warren's choice of precedents for *Brown* (II) might suggest that there were no cases available that were more appropriate; such was not true, however. Although there are no precedents in equity to support the *psychological* understanding of equality in *Brown* (I) or the *sociological* understanding of equity in *Brown* (II), there are a substantial number of cases to support the exercise of the equity power in defense of constitutional rights. The citation of any of these cases would have added a greater air of judicial consistency to the School Desegregation Implementation Case than did *Alexander* v. *Hillman* and *Hecht* v. *Bowles.*

As early as 1824, in *Osborn* v. *the Bank of the United States,* the Court held that a federal court "in a proper case in equity, may enjoin a State officer from executing a state law in conflict with the Constitution or a statute of the United States, when such execution will violate the rights of the complainant" (at 858, 859, 868).[12] And in 1871, in *Johnson* v. *Towsley,* the Court proclaimed that courts of equity have the power to inquire into and correct mistakes, injustice, and wrong in legislative and executive action when it invades private rights. This concept, of equitable relief being appropriate in cases of constitutional deprivation, began to take on added significance after the Civil War and Reconstruction.

In 1912 the Court found in *Philadelphia* v. *Stimson* that

> where an officer is proceeding under an unconstitutional act, its invalidity suffices to show that he is without authority and this absence of lawful power and his abuse of authority in imposing or enforcing, in the name of the state unwarrantable extractions or restrictions to the

irreparable loss of the complainant forms the basis of a decree in equity. [At 605][13]

In spite of a lingering belief that the jurisdiction of equity was "limited to the rights of property,"[14] the Court was beginning to take the view that deprivation of any constitutional right might be sufficient to constitute an irreparable injury for which the complainant could appeal to equitable principles. In 1915 a case that reached the Supreme Court alleged that an Arizona law restricting the number of aliens an employer could hire, relative to the number of citizens employed, was a violation of the equal protection of the laws guaranteed by the Fourteenth Amendment. In this case—*Truax* v. *Raich*—Chief Justice Hughes, writing for the Court, pointed out that such an act precluded a remedy at law, and, since it was "entirely clear that unless the enforcement of the act is restrained the complainant will have no adequate remedy [and since] the unconstitutionality of the act is shown, equitable relief may be had" (at 39). Granting that it was within the power of state legislatures to make "reasonable classifications" among citizens, the Court denied that this power extended so far as to enable a state to deny the equal protection of the laws to its lawful inhabitants "because of their race or nationality." In this instance, the right being denied the aliens was the right to enjoy the ordinary means of earning a livelihood. Should such discrimination be permitted, Hughes concluded, "solely upon the ground of race or nationality, the prohibition of the denial to any person of the equal protection of the laws would be a barren form of words" (at 41).

In *Terrace* v. *Thompson* the Court, speaking through Mr. Justice Butler, expanded the *Truax* rule by insisting that complainants who allege that a state act is "repugnant to the due process and equal protection clauses of the Fourteenth Amendment" need not be "obliged to take the risk of prosecution, fines, and imprisonment and loss of property in order to secure an adjudication of their rights. The complainant presents a case in which equitable relief may be had, if the law complained of is shown to be in contravention of the Federal Constitution" (at 215–16). In these cases—*Osborn, Stimson, Johnson, Truax,* and *Terrace*—however, there still remained a factual link between the suit in equity and loss of property.

It was not until 1939 that the Court finally acknowledged that there need not be any jurisdictional amount of loss to the complainant before a case can be brought in equity on the ground of constitutional deprivation. In *Hague* v. *Committee for Industrial Organization* a suit was brought praying an injunction to enjoin the enforcement of a local ordinance that permitted the director of public safety to deny a permit for any assembly that in his judgment might lead to "riots, disturbances, or disorderly assemblage." Not surprisingly, the most cogent arguments on the question of equity jurisdiction are set forth in Mr. Justice Stone's concurring opinion.

Following the Court's decision in *In re Sawyer*, it had generally been held as accepted law that "unless enlarged by express statute" the jurisdiction of equity was confined to the adjudication of property rights. In his opinion in *Hague*, Stone pointed to such an "express statute"—the Civil Rights Act of 1871. According to the first section of that legislation, any citizen could bring a suit in equity to restrain the infringement of rights guaranteed to all citizens by the due process clause of the Fourteenth Amendment. In 1875 an act of Congress had subsequently established a jurisdictional amount of $3,000 for cases brought in equity. To Stone, the latter act in no way required a plaintiff to "allege and prove that the Constitutional immunity he seeks to vindicate has a value in excess of $3,000" (at 529). He explained further:

There are many rights and immunities secured by the Constitution, of which freedom of speech and assembly are conspicuous examples, which are not capable of money valuation, and in many instances, like the present, no suit in equity could be maintained for their protection if proof of the jurisdictional amount were prerequisite.

Continuing, Stone observed:

The conclusion seems inescapable that the right conferred by the Act of 1871 to maintain a suit in equity in the federal courts to protect the suitor against a deprivation of rights or immunities secured by the Constitution, has been preserved, and whenever the right or immunity is one of personal liberty, not dependent upon the infringement of property rights, there is jurisdiction in the District Court under S.24(14) of the Judicial Code to entertain it without proof that the amount in controversy exceeds $3,000. [At 531–32]

It seems strange that Mr. Chief Justice Warren somehow disregarded these cases in his opinion in *Brown* (II). Moreover, there were other cases, of an even more expansive nature concerning the limits of equity, that would have made a stronger precedential foundation for his expansive assertion of the powers of equity than did either *Alexander* v. *Hillman* or *Hecht* v. *Bowles*.

In an 1896 case, *Union Pacific Railroad Co.* v. *Chicago, R.I. & P.R. Co.*, the Court had asserted that equity had always been characterized by "flexibility and expansiveness, so that new remedies may be invented or old ones modified in order to meet the requirements of every case and to satisfy the needs of a progressive social condition" (at 564). This thought was vastly expanded in *Porter* v. *Warner*, a case which, like *Hecht*, concerned the Emergency Price Control Act. In many ways *Porter* v. *Warner* would have been a perfect precedent from the point of view of Warren's opinion. Citing, as Warren did, *Hecht* v. *Bowles,* Mr. Justice Murphy expounded thus:

> Unless otherwise provided [for] by statute, all the inherent equitable powers of the District Court are available for the proper and complete exercise of that jurisdiction. And since the public interest is involved in a proceeding of this nature, those equitable powers assume a broader and more flexible character than when only a private controversy is at stake. Power is thereby resident in the District Court in exercising this jurisdiction "to do equity and to mould each decree to the necessities of the particular case." It may act also so as to adjust and reconcile competing claims and so as to accord full justice to all the real parties in interest; if necessary, persons not originally connected with the litigation may be brought before the Court so that their rights in the subject-matter may be determined and enforced. [At 398][15]

There is, of course, no way, short of an explicit statement by Warren, of knowing why he chose *Alexander* v. *Hillman* and *Hecht* v. *Bowles* as precedents when seemingly more appropriate cases were available. It seems fair to say, however, that he could have marshaled more compelling precedential law to his cause than he did. But even the more appropriate cases cited here had never approached the massive expansion of federal equity powers at the expense of the tradition of the principles of equity jurisprudence to the extent that Warren expanded them in *Brown* (II). The cases he chose not to use would only have lent a degree of judicial consistency to his project; they could not have lent it any degree of jurisprudential legitimacy. For the *Brown* (II) opinion constituted a powerful assault against some of the most substantial principles of equity jurisprudence—principles that had prevented the equity power from becoming little more than a means of expressing the judicial will.

III

In order to proclaim the new application and understanding of equity in *Brown* (II), Chief Justice Warren was forced to ignore much of the vast tradition of equitable principles that had developed in America from the time of the Founding. At the birth of the republic in 1789, it was believed that the equity power of the federal courts would be a safe complement to the established republican political order so long as it was bound down by precedent and hemmed in by rules and procedures. Since the young country had not established a body of precedent, its lawmakers looked to English experience. In 1792, in *Hayburn's Case,* the Supreme Court announced the first "rules" with which it would govern federal equity. It would, the Court said, be guided by the practice of the Court of "*Chancery* in England, as affording outlines for the practice of this court"; further, it would "from time to time" make any alterations necessary to the peculiar political system of America (at 413–14). This reliance on the English model received its classic expression in 1818. The Court, in *Robinson* v. *Campbell,* reaffirmed that "the remedies in the courts of the United States are to be, at common law or in equity . . . according to the principles of the common law and equity as distinguished and defined in that country from which we derive our knowledge of those principles" (at 223).[16] Every federal court in every state was to be so guided.[17] Although the Constitution vested in Congress the power to ordain and establish inferior courts and thereby the "power to prescribe and regulate the modes of proceeding in such Courts,"[18] it generally delegated such rule-making to the Supreme Court, subject to congressional approval. And the Supreme Court continued to take as its guide in such matters the English principles of equity jurisprudence.

The most fundamental equity maxim embraced by the federal judiciary in the first century of our national experience was the separation of law and equity. Mr. Justice Wayne in *Brown* v. *Swann* gave what is perhaps the earliest and clearest judicial expression of this maxim:

> Courts of Chancery have . . . established rules for the exercise of this jurisdiction to keep it within its proper limits, and to prevent it from encroaching upon the jurisdiction of the courts of common law. [At 501]

Thus the early Court was willing to exercise a healthy self-restraint and keep from stepping into its "shoes of equity" whenever it found that the law restrained it from giving an opinion.[19] Maintaining a deep reverence for the "established doctrines and settled principles of equity," it upheld, even in the face of growing pressure from the Codification Movement, the necessity of strict separation of law and equity in the federal judiciary. The justices tended to eschew "arbitrary and capricious"[20] discretion in favor of what Joseph Story called "judicial discretion"[21]—discretion guided by a reverence for precedent.

This reverence for precedent tended to preclude any extension of equity jurisdiction whenever an "adequate, complete, and plain remedy" existed at law. Within its remedial area, a court of equity's jurisdiction was "as well defined and limited as is that of a court of law." It was bound, ultimately, to follow the law. A court of equity had no control over "imperfect obligations, resting upon conscience and moral duty only, unconnected with legal obligations." Mr. Justice Hunt, in *Rees* v. *Watertown*, elaborated this point.

> Generally, its jurisdiction depends upon legal obligations, and its decrees can only enforce remedies to the extent and in the mode by law established.
>
> A court of equity cannot by avowing that there is a right but no remedy known to the law create a remedy in violation of law, or even without the authority of law. It acts upon established principles not only, but through established channels. [At 122]

When the law provides a remedy that is adequate and complete, an equity court has no authority to embellish or replace it: "time and the law must perfect its execution" (at 125). To assert that courts of equity had the power to vindicate abstract principles of justice[22] would have been viewed as an invitation to leave the courts to a "dangerous discretion, and to roam at large in the trackless field of their own imaginations."[23]

Even after the enthusiasm for codification's cardinal tenet of simplification had infected the Supreme Court and Congress, there lingered among the justices a faith in the substantive difference between law and equity. The Law and Equity Act of 1915—which allowed action begun on either side of the court to be transferred to the other side without the necessity of commencing a new action to permit determination-of-law questions to arise in equity actions and to allow equitable defenses to be offered and equitable relief to be granted in an action at law—was held not to have altered the substance of equity.[24] When the momentum of the effort to reform civil procedure peaked in 1938 with the new Rules of Civil Procedure, it was subsequently conceded by the Court that the collapse of the distinction between law and equity had "rendered anachronistic the technical niceties"[25] that had distinguished the two jurisdictions. But as late as 1949, the Court still insisted that, "notwithstanding the fusion of law and equity in the Rules of Civil Procedure, the substantive principles of courts of chancery remain unaffected."[26]

Related to the maxim that equity jurisdiction was prohibited when there was an adequate and complete remedy at law[27] was the understanding that, to be cognizable in a court of equity, an injury had to be irreparable;[28] if it was not clearly irreparable, even though the offending law or statute was either illegal or unconstitutional, equity would not interfere.[29] Mr. Justice Swayne in 1862 clarified the irreparable-injury requirement, asserting that

> A Court of Equity will interfere when the injury by the wrongful act of the adverse party will be irreparable, as where the loss of health, the

107

loss of trade, the destruction of the means of subsistence, or the ruin of property must ensue.[30]

This was not in any sense an expansion of equity jurisdiction, for, to claim irreparable injury, the complainant needed proof: "The mere assertion that the apprehended acts will inflict irreparable injury is not enough. Facts must be alleged from which the court can reasonably infer that such would be the result."[31] The prerequisites for claiming irreparable injury were rigid. Even when no adequate remedy at law existed, that fact in no way guaranteed access to the equity jurisdiction. As Mr. Justice Miller observed in *Heine* v. *the Levee Commissioners*,

> the hardship of the case, and the failure of the mode of procedure
> established at law, is not sufficient to justify a court of equity to depart
> from all precedent and assume an unregulated power of administering
> abstract justice at the expense of well-settled principles. [At 658]

This restrictive maxim was reaffirmed in 1939 by Mr. Justice Stone. "Absence of a legal remedy," he wrote, "does not dispense with the necessity of alleging and proving a cause of action in equity as a prerequisite to equitable relief in a federal court."[32]

The American concept of federalism also exerted a great influence on equity jurisprudence. Throughout its equity opinions the Supreme Court generally deferred to the sanctity of the structure of the federal system. It was generally believed that an injunction ought not to issue against officers of a state empowered to enforce the law being questioned unless the case was "reasonably free from doubt" and the "danger of irreparable loss [was] both great and immediate."[33] To issue such an injunction would be "improvident" as well as "beyond the proper discretion of the Court."[34] It was necessary that the Court maintain a "scrupulous regard for the rightful independence of state governments . . . in every case where the asserted federal right may be preserved without . . . the extraordinary remedies of equity."[35] Mr. Justice Cardozo perhaps said it best:

> Caution and reluctance there must be in special measure where relief,
> if granted, is an interference by the process of injunction with the ac-
> tivities of state officers discharging in good faith their supposed duties.
>   Only a case of manifest oppression will justify a federal court in
> laying such a check upon administrative officers acting *colore officii* in
> a conscientious endeavor to fulfill their duty to the state. A prudent
> self-restraint is called for at such times if state and national functions
> are to be maintained in stable equilibrium.[36]

It was generally considered "in the public interest that federal courts of equity should exercise their discretionary power with proper regard for the rightful independence of state governments in carrying out their domestic policy."[37] Even the unconstitutionality of a state law was insufficient to invoke the "extraordinary power of a court of equity," because the preservation of the "autonomy of the states" was considered "fundamental" under the American Constitution.[38]

Given these "traditional attributes of equity," it seems astonishing—indeed, incredible—that Mr. Chief Justice Warren in *Brown* (II) could have asserted the doctrine of equitable relief as he did. Certainly, as we have noted, a line of judicial opinion was developing that held unconstitutional state laws to be adequate proof of irreparable injury to the complainant. But, even on the basis of *Hague*, "a feeling of inferiority" seems a woefully inadequate injury; it seems even weaker when compared with the freedom-of-speech and freedom-of-assembly questions addressed by the Court in *Hague*. Moreover, those two constitutional rights are concretely stated in the First Amendment. When Warren asserted that such a "*feeling* of inferiority...*may* affect their hearts and minds in a way *unlikely* ever to be undone" (*Brown* I, at 494; italics added), he effectively, in light of the equitable principle of irreparable injury, introduced enough doubt and ambiguity to demand rejection of the case as a suit in equity.

Education was perhaps, as Warren suggested, "the most important function of state and local governments" (at 493). Surely it was a matter of state law, and to administer that law on an unequal basis violated the prohibition against the states' denying the equal protection of its laws to all citizens. But it is not clear that separate schools—equally funded and equally provided for—as in the Kansas situation, could not, *on the basis of the Constitution* and without a resort to "conscience" or a sense of "moral duty," satisfy that requirement.[39]

But, even granting the legitimacy of *Brown* (I) in declaring racial separation to violate *in principle* the Equal Protection Clause (which, on the basis of the constitutional law of *Truax* v. *Raich, Terrace* v. *Thompson,* and Mr. Justice Harlan's dissent in *Plessy* v. *Ferguson,* could have been soundly decided), it does not follow that the Court could legitimately do any more than enjoin the enforcement of the state laws in question. Educational policy, being reserved to the states, was not within the realm of federal authority and certainly not within the realm of judicial competence. Having enjoined the further enforcement of the state laws, Warren could have left the remedy to law, administered by the state governments, or, failing that, to federal legislation, such as the existing Civil Rights Acts.

To order the transformation of "racially discriminatory" schools with "all deliberate speed" abandoned the entire tradition of American equity jurisprudence. The stipulation that the district courts would be responsible for determining whether the local authorities were complying with the order would demand that the courts endeavor to superintend a decree so vast that the courts in essence assumed a legislative function,[40] thus setting the stage for future judicial intrusions. The high court's venture into the realm of educational policy would be unprecedented in scale.

IV

In *The Nature of the Judicial Process,* Benjamin N. Cardozo aptly pointed out that one aspect of the judicial process is the "historical method, or the method of evolution." The heart of this method is the understanding that there is always present in judicial opinions the "tendency of a principle to expand itself to the limit of its logic."[41] This expansive tendency is particularly a problem when the principle evoked is as theoretically, historically, and politically flawed as Chief Justice Warren's equitable-implementation opinion was in the second *Brown* case.

In the *Brown* (II) opinion, the Chief Justice planted the seed of the new sociological understanding of equity, which took as its primary concern the social class or group instead of the individual. In subsequent opinions this new idea would be brought to fruition in the form of relieving against both *de jure* and *de facto* segregation and granting relief to those groups suffering the effects of "past discrimination." And in each opinion based on the *Brown* equity principle, the Court would become more and more embroiled in the "sensitive areas of social policy."[42]

Seven   The Descendants of *Brown:*
The Perpetuation of a Bad Idea

The standard for equitable relief set by the Supreme Court in *Brown* (II) was itself indicative of the theoretical poverty of the sociological equity concept Chief Justice Warren had formulated. "The District Courts [are] to take such proceedings and enter such orders and decrees consistent with this opinion," the Chief Justice said, "as are necessary and proper to admit to public schools on a racially nondiscriminatory basis *with all deliberate speed* the parties to these cases" (at 301; italics added). The demand that desegregation be pursued "with all deliberate speed" was vague. The complainants had been adjudged psychologically injured by a deprivation by the states of their constitutionally guaranteed rights, but relief was not to be immediate. The reason was clear. Although the Court had denied the relevance of the particular circumstances of the four separate cases when they reached the "unifying legal question" in *Brown* (I), they were forced in *Brown* (II) to take account of those peculiar circumstances in providing relief. To have done otherwise, and to have promulgated nationwide relief, would have been to formulate policy on a grander scale than the Court in 1955 was willing to do. As a result, the recalcitrant states used stalling tactics or outright resistance to thwart relief for an injury assertedly uniform in character.

For more than a decade, compliance with the *Brown* (II) decree remained more a wish than a reality.[1] In the meantime, however, the Court continued to expand the *Brown* (I) principle prohibiting

111

racial discrimination. In 1958 it reached to public parks and golf courses,[2] in 1959 to athletic events,[3] in 1962 to service in airport restaurants.[4] In 1963 the rule was stretched to cover seating in courtrooms,[5] and in 1964 it extended to the use of a municipal auditorium.[6]

Following the Court's lead, Congress adopted as the national standard a policy on nondiscrimination. By the Civil Rights Act of 1964 not only education but employment, public accommodations and facilities, and federally assisted programs were to be administered on a nondiscriminatory basis.

The road to the Civil Rights Act of 1964 had been a rough one for its proponents.[7] They were constantly called on to assure opponents of the bill that the law could never be used by any court or administrative agency to *demand* integration—in contradistinction to *prohibiting* segregation—by setting standards for racial mixing. The debates in Congress clearly illustrate that the proponents of the legislation firmly believed that that would never occur. To defend their position and to assuage the suspicions of the opposition, the leadership brought to their support a lower federal court opinion that, on appeal, had been denied *certiorari* by the Supreme Court and hence upheld. In *Bell* v. *City School of Gary, Indiana,* the Court had held that

> Desegregation does not mean that there must be intermingling of the races in all school districts. It means only that they may not be prevented from intermingling or going to school together because of race or color. [At 213]

In denying *certiorari,* the Supreme Court had in essence approved the notion of assignment to a neighborhood school in spite of the fact that "the resulting effect is to have racial imbalance in certain schools where the district is populated almost entirely by Negroes or whites." To further allay the fears of the unconvinced representatives and senators, the bill as adopted included clauses clearly stating the limited objectives of the legislation.[8] The Civil Rights Act of 1964 included the following restrictions in Section 2000c of Title IV:

> "Desegregation" means the assignment of students to public schools and within such schools without regard to their race, color, religion, or national origin, but "desegregation" shall not mean the assignment of students to public schools in order to overcome racial imbalance.

In authorizing the attorney general to institute federal suits, Section 2000c went further:

> . . . nothing herein shall empower any official or court of the United States to issue any order seeking to achieve a racial balance in any

school by requiring the transportation of pupils or students from one school to another or one school district to another in order to achieve such racial balance, or otherwise enlarge the existing power of the court to insure compliance with constitutional standards.[9]

However, when the Office of Education of the Department of Health, Education, and Welfare set out, in 1966, to formulate guidelines[10] for the implementation of the Civil Rights Act of 1964, the original *prohibition* of segregation gradually evolved—through a dialectical administrative and judicial process—into a *demand* for full integration,[11] in spite of the clearly stated intention of the legislators. In time the Supreme Court would elevate this bureaucratic "suggestion" for integration to the level of constitutional principle, thereby depriving Congress of any immediate control over the question of racial separation in the schools.

I

By 1963, cases began to reach the Supreme Court in which the original guideline of "all deliberate speed" was replaced by "at once." The first warning that time for the "all deliberate speed" doctrine was running out came in *Goss* v. *Board of Education of Knoxville, Tennessee,* where the Court admonished as follows:

> Now . . . eight years after this [*Brown* (II)] decree was rendered, and over nine years from the first *Brown* decision, the context in which we must interpret and apply this language to plans for desegregation has been significantly altered. [At 689]

A year later the Court made the point even more explicit. In *Griffin* v. *County School Board of Prince Edward County, Virginia,* it declared that "the time for mere 'deliberate speed' has run out" (at 234). Delays in implementing *Brown* became, in a 1965 case, "no longer tolerable."[12] Then in 1967, the Court, by denying *certiorari,* upheld a lower court's decision that presented a radical departure from the *Brown* principle.

In *United States* v. *Jefferson County Board of Education*[13] Judge John Minor Wisdom dismissed any distinction between "desegregation" and "integration" as merely "a quibble devised over ten years ago by a misreading of *Brown.*" To Judge Wisdom (and, apparently, to the Supreme Court) it was clear that "the United States Constitution, as construed in *Brown,* requires public school systems to integrate students, faculties, facilities, and activities" and that the laws made pursuant thereto imposed "an absolute duty to integrate." To Judge Wisdom and the Supreme Court, racial mixing of students had become—in opposition to the clearly stated provisions of the Civil Rights Act of 1964—"a high priority educational goal" (at 845–46).[14]

113

The lower court, during a rehearing of the case *en banc*, upheld the ruling but was bitterly divided.[15] Judge Walter Gewin was unambiguous in his dissent:

> Whenever concepts as to proportions and percentages are imposed on school systems, notwithstanding free choices actually made, we have destroyed freedom and liberty by judicial fiat; and even worse, we have done so in the very name of that liberty and freedom we so avidly claim to espouse.... Both proportional representation and proportional limitation are equally unconstitutional. [At 397, 404, 405]

Judge Griffin Bell was also not blind to the judicial sleight-of-hand that Judge Wisdom had performed. He observed that any "mandatory assignment of students based on race" was a "new and drastic doctrine" that threw "new fuel" on an "old fire" that had yet to be brought under control. "It is unthinkable," he ruminated, "that our Constitution does not contemplate a middle ground—no compulsion one way or the other" (at 414). The Constitution was not, after all, color-blind, as Judge James Colman pointed out. The thrust of *Jefferson County*, Colman argued, was to deny "the freedom of the Negro child to attend any public school without regard to his race or color." For Judge Colman, as for his dissenting brethren, Judges Bell and Gewin, the implications of the case were clear:

> Because of his race [the Negro child] can be assigned to a particular school to achieve a result satisfactory to someone who probably does not even live in the district but who wishes to make a racial point. [At 419–20]

Judge John Godbold prophetically summed up his dissent by warning that "Courts are the prisoners of their own slogans, and the dictum of today is to be asserted as the law of tomorrow" (at 421).

In 1968 the Court handed down an opinion that made explicit the implications of the new idea of equitable relief formulated in *Brown* (II). In one sense, *Green* v. *County School Board of New Kent County* was a radical departure—from the prohibition *against* racial segregation in *Brown* (I) to a new affirmative demand *for* racial integration—but in another sense it was merely the fulfillment of the logic of the new idea of sociological equity that *Brown* (II) had presented.

II

The *Green* case addressed the question whether "freedom of choice" plans—plans enabling students to attend the school of their choice without encountering racial barriers—were adequate to the remedial demands of *Brown* (II). Such freedom-of-choice plans had sprung up throughout the South in response to the *Brown* (II) decree but had generally come far short of producing anything resembling a unitary school system.

In the case of the schools of New Kent County, presented in *Green,* no white student, after three years of freedom of choice, had chosen to attend the formerly all black school, where nearly 85 percent of the black students in the county remained. The opponents of the desegregation plan argued that the schools in the county remained "racially identifiable" and that it was abolition of such racial identity that the *Brown* (II) decision demanded. The school board of New Kent County argued that its freedom-of-choice plan could "be faulted only by reading the Fourteenth Amendment as universally requiring 'compulsory' integration." The Court was unconvinced. That argument, Mr. Justice Brennan wrote (at 431), "ignores the thrust of *Brown* (II). In the light of the command of that case, what is involved here is the question whether the Board has achieved the 'racially nondiscriminatory school system' *Brown* (II) held must be effectuated in order to remedy the established unconstitutional deficiencies of its segregated system." Thus, the demand in *Brown* (II) (at 299) for a "good faith implementation of the Constitutional principles" of *Brown* (I) was no longer sufficient; results were now necessary. And the only result the Court would be willing to accept would be an immediate conversion to "a unitary system in which racial discrimination would be eliminated root and branch." "The burden on a school board today," Brennan continued, "is to come forward with a plan that promises realistically to work, and promises realistically to work *now*" (*Green,* at 438–39).

Lest state and local authorities forget who was to judge future plans for integration, the Court reaffirmed the provisions of *Brown* (II). Citing *Louisiana* v. *United States,* Brennan extended the *Brown* (II) claim of equity jurisdiction to an assertion of moral obligation:

> We bear in mind that the Court has not merely the power but the duty to render a decree which will so far as possible eliminate the discriminatory effects of the past as well as bar like discrimination in the future. [*Louisiana,* at 154; cited in *Green,* at 438]

It seemed clear to the Court that "whatever plan is adopted will require evaluation in practice, and the court should retain jurisdiction until it is clear that state-imposed segregation has been completely removed" (at 439).

The *Green* opinion left no doubt that the mandate of *Brown* had little to do with freedom: "freedom of choice is not an end in itself" (at 440). The problem, of course, was that freedom of choice had been for quite some time an end in itself. For the freedom to choose is based on a fundamental respect for the individual and his ability to decide what is in his best interest. The fact that roughly 15 percent of the black students of New Kent County had chosen, and been permitted, to attend the formerly all-white school indicated that the *de jure* system of segregation in New Kent County had been effectively weakened. It was not clear that the 85 percent who had remained in their original school were simply not "courageous enough to break with tradition" and seek a place in the white school; it may have been the case that they simply preferred to stay in the old school, where, presumably, they felt comfortable.

In the history of the desegregation cases, *Green* clearly "marked the end of the Supreme Court's reticence on questions of race and the schools." As Lino A. Graglia has pointed out, "Decisions now came rapidly and easily. No obstacle to greater integration, it seemed, could longer exist; no further requirement to achieve integration could be too severe or too soon imposed."[16]

The Court followed *Green* a year later with *United States* v. *Montgomery County Board of Education.* Under *Brown* (II), Mr. Justice Black observed for a unanimous Court, the Court was not content to leave the task of desegregation in the "unsupervised hands of local school authorities, trained as most would be under the old laws and practices, with loyalties to the system of separate white and Negro schools" (at 227). If Negro children were to receive their constitutional rights, Black insisted, "the coercive assistance of the courts was imperatively called for" (at 228). Black concluded that "specific commands" are often necessary and always permissible under the remedial power of the Court and that a federal district judge was hence empowered to order the Montgomery, Alabama, County Board of Education to desegregate faculty and staff according to a specific mathematical ratio (at 235).

In *Alexander* v. *Holmes County Board of Education,* four months after *Montgomery,* Mr. Justice Black spoke again for a unanimous Court. "All deliberate speed," he insisted, was "no longer constitutionally permissible." Citing *Green,* he declared that, by the order of the Court, "the obligation of every school district is to terminate dual school systems at once and to operate now and hereafter only unitary schools" (at 20).

The Court had overcome its original inertia and was now willing to uphold remedies of nearly every sort. In 1970, in *Carter* v. *West Feliciana Parish Schools,* the Court overruled the Fifth Circuit Court of Appeals, which had held that the "merger of student bodies into unitary systems" was inherently "difficult to arrange" and that the school system could therefore postpone pupil reassignment until the next term.[17] Not so, the Supreme Court ruled; "at once" meant "immediately," and no further delays would be tolerated. Therefore, it was constitutionally required that the school board arrange for the mid-term transfer of students in order to achieve what the Court viewed as a properly integrated school system.

On the basis of the *Green* opinion the Court had, in *Alexander* and *Carter,* rendered remedies that can be described only as drastic. The Supreme Court, traditionally understood as providing a restraint on the governmental excesses of the other branches, was beginning to emerge as perhaps the "most dangerous source of excess."[18] The excess of the Supreme Court stemmed from its attempt to do more than restrain government officials from infringing the constitutional rights of the citizens. It was attempting—beginning with *Brown* (II)—to give relief—a remedy— that went beyond an injunction (itself an extraordinary power of equity); the Court was seeking to assuage the effects of past wrongs in much the same way a monetary remedy might be decreed in other equity suits. But however excessive the Court's remedies in *Alexander* and *Carter* had been, they would be nearly lost in the shadow cast by the Court's next major foray into the realm of educational policy: *Swann* v. *Charlotte-Mecklenburg County Board of Education.*

III

In *Swann,* the Supreme Court for the first time attempted to offer a sustained defense of the *Brown* (II) equity principle. This was necessary because, after the *Brown* (II) ruling, the lower courts had been left to "grapple with the flinty, intractable, realities of day-to-day implementation." As a result, the lower courts had been forced to "improvise and experiment without detailed or specific guidelines." Consequently, "their efforts, of necessity, embraced a process of 'trial and error'" (at 6).

At first, the unanimous opinion of the Court, written by Mr. Chief Justice Burger, seemed to be pointing toward some restriction on the equitable remedies permissible under *Brown* (II). But, the more he wrote, the more obvious it became that restriction had nothing to do with this opinion. "The problems encountered by the district courts and courts of appeal," Burger pointed out, "make plain that we should now try to amplify guidelines, *however incomplete and imperfect,* for the assistance of school authorities and courts" (at 16; italics added). But, even though, he continued, "no fixed or even substantially fixed guidelines can be established as to how far a court can go . . . it must be recognized that there are limits" (at 28). However, this opinion touched on boundaries in a limited way. The Court was not really attempting to fashion strict guidelines; it was, rather, attempting to show that the inherent equity powers of the federal courts were in fact nearly unlimited.

The objective was to eliminate "all vestiges of state-imposed segrega-

117

tion'' in the public schools. If, under the mandates of *Brown* and *Green,* local authorities fail in their ''affirmative obligations'' to abolish their dual school systems, then ''judicial authority may be invoked'' (at 28). Citing *Hecht,* Burger then presented the kernel of the *Swann* ruling:

> Once a right and a violation have been shown, the scope of a district court's equitable powers to remedy past wrongs is broad, for breadth and flexibility are inherent in equitable remedies [and] a school de-segregation case does not differ fundamentally from other cases involving the framing of equitable remedies to repair the denial of a constitutional right. The task is to correct, by a balancing of the individual and collective interests, the condition that offends the Constitution.

Continuing:

> In seeking to define even in broad and general terms how far this remedial power extends it is important to remember that judicial powers may be exercised only on the basis of a constitutional violation. Remedial judicial authority does not put judges automatically in the shoes of school authorities whose powers are plenary. Judicial authority enters only when local authority defaults.

The Chief Justice concluded this part of his argument as follows:

> As with any equity case, the nature of the violation determines the scope of the remedy. In default by the School authorities of their obligation to proffer acceptable remedies, a district court has broad power to fashion a remedy that will assure a unitary school system. [At 15–16]

Having established the inherently broad limits of the federal equity power, the Chief Justice then turned to the specific claim by the school authorities that the equity powers of the federal district courts had been limited by the Civil Rights Act of 1964 (Section 2000, quoted above). Burger concluded that the provisions of the 1964 legislation were to be read only as not granting *new* powers; there was no suggestion, he insisted, that the Congress intended to withdraw or restrict any of the ''historic equitable remedial powers'' of the federal courts (at 17). ''In sum,'' Burger observed, ''the very limited use made of mathematical ratios was within the equitable remedial discretion of the District Court'' (at 25). The Court recognized that such remedies may be ''administratively awkward, inconvenient, and even bizarre'' but insisted that ''all awkwardness and inconvenience cannot be avoided in the interim period when remedial adjustments are being made to eliminate the dual school systems'' (at 28). The Supreme Court had now explicitly endorsed the dictum of Judge Minor Wisdom in the *Jefferson County* case; integration had indeed become "a high priority educational goal."

Despite its stated intention to offer guidelines for equitable relief in future desegregation cases, the Court in *Swann* only further weakened whatever significance precedent and principle still retained in such cases. That the Court was unable to provide any reasoned defense of the equity power in desegregation suits was made clear by Chief Justice Burger's closing dictum—a statement that no doubt would have stunned such jurists as Joseph Story, Harlan Fiske Stone, and Felix Frankfurter. Burger asserted that,

> in seeking to define the scope of remedial power or the limits on re-medial power of courts in an area as sensitive as we deal with here, words are poor instruments to convey the sense of basic fairness in-herent in equity. Substance, not semantics, must govern, and we have sought to suggest the nature of limitations without frustrating the ap-propriate scope of equity. [At 31]

What had begun to emerge in *Green, Montgomery, Alexander,* and *Carter* was in plain view: the federal district courts were, by the "author-ity" of the Supreme Court, to be in effect the surrogate school boards of the nation.

After *Swann* the desegregation cases reaching the Supreme Court con-tinued unabated, and in each subsequent case the borders of equitable relief were extended farther and farther. In 1972 the Court decreed that a federal court can halt state or local action creating a new school district when the effect would be to impede desegregation.[19] In 1973 an evenly divided Court overturned a federal court order that had directed school officials of the predominantly black Richmond, Virginia, school district to consolidate with neighboring white-majority county systems in order to desegregate the city system. When newly appointed Justice Lewis Pow-ell, a native Virginian, took no part in the case, the result was to leave intact the Fourth Circuit Court's reversal of the district court order.[20] Then, in 1973, the Supreme Court, taking its policy of forced integration north and west, handed down a startling opinion in *Keyes* v. *School District No. 1, Denver, Colorado.*

While paying lip service to the *de jure/de facto* distinction in desegrega-tion cases, the Court, speaking through Mr. Justice Brennan, essentially obliterated that distinction. The distinguishing factor between *de jure* and *de facto* segregation was held to be "*purpose* or *intent* to segregate" (at 208). In the Denver system, which had never been operated under a constitutional or statutory provision that mandated or permitted racial segregation in public education, the burden was on the school officials to prove their innocence. Brennan wrote:

> In discharging that burden, it is not enough, of course, that the school authorities rely upon some allegedly logical, racially neutral explanation for their actions. Their burden is to adduce proof sufficient to support a finding that segregative intent was not among the factors that motivated their actions. [At 210]

Failure to provide sufficient proof was, on the basis of *Swann,* sufficient cause to invoke the remedial powers of the federal judiciary, and it was soon to be made clear that future remedies would go even farther than court-ordered busing.

In a unanimous opinion in 1974, *Lau* v. *Nichols,* the Court decreed that, under the Civil Rights Act of 1964, school officials have an affirmative obligation to provide non-English-speaking students in their system with remedial instruction in the English language.

Also in 1974, the Court in *Milliken* v. *Bradley* (I) returned to the issue that had been presented in *Bradley* v. *State Board of Education of the Commonwealth of Virginia:* whether a multidistrict remedy for school segregation is within the remedial powers of the federal courts. The Court now, in a five-to-four decision (Mr. Justice Powell thereby indicating how the Richmond case would have been decided had he participated), denied the lower court's order for interdistrict busing to relieve segregation. But, while denying it in this instance, the Court left the door open by admitting that "an interdistrict remedy might be in order where the racially discriminatory acts of one or more school districts caused racial segregation in an adjacent district, or where district lines have been deliberately drawn on the basis of race" (at 745). In 1976 the Court blundered through that door in *Hills* v. *Gautreaux,* upholding a decree for metropolitan-wide relief for housing discrimination in Chicago. Stewart held that "there is no basis for the . . . claim that court-ordered metropolitan relief . . . would be impermissible as a matter of law under the *Milliken* decision" (at 305).

In spite of the *Hills* opinion, there came during 1976 a hint that there might actually be some limitation on the equitable powers of the federal judiciary. In *Pasadena City Board of Education* v. *Spangler* Mr. Justice Rehnquist, writing for a six-man majority (Brennan and Marshall dissenting, Stevens not participating), held that the District Court, in enforcing its order to require annual readjustment of attendance zones once the school board had successfully established a racially neutral system of student assignment, had "exceeded its authority" (at 435). As though to make certain that no one would assume the equity powers were too limited, the Court during the next term returned to its expansive position.

The Descendants of *Brown:*
The Perpetuation of a Bad Idea

In the second *Milliken* v. *Bradley* case the Supreme Court endeavored once again to grapple with the vexatious problem of equitable relief in desegregation suits, and its decision essentially plowed under the last vestiges of restraint in granting remedies. Chief Justice Burger said:

> In a word, discriminatory student policies can themselves manifest and breed other inequalities built into a dual system founded on racial discrimination. Federal courts need not, and cannot, close their eyes to inequalities, shown by the record, which flow from a long standing segregated system.

Continuing:

> Children who have been thus educationally and culturally set apart from the larger community will inevitably acquire habits of speech, conduct, and attitudes reflecting their cultural isolation.

Therefore, concluded Burger:

> Pupil assignment alone does not automatically remedy the impact of previous, unlawful educational isolation; the consequences linger and can be dealt with only by independent measures . . . ; the root condition shown by this record must be treated directly by special training at the hands of teachers prepared for that task. [At 283, 287, 288]

Thus, in language reminiscent of the original *Brown* decision, the Supreme Court twenty years later continued to cling to its psychological understanding of equality and its sociological understanding of equitable relief.

IV

The problem presented by this new understanding of equality and equity is that the Court continues to operate under two mistaken assumptions. First, the Court assumes that it has the institutional capacity to deal with such issues; second, it assumes and asserts that it has the constitutional power to do so. To see that the first assumption is erroneous, one need only consider the lack of consistency in the Court's decisions as well as its continued reliance on sociological and psychological research for its standard of constitutional meaning. To see that the second assumption, of constitutional legitimacy, is equally fallacious, one need only look to the great tradition of equity jurisprudence and, in particular, to the history of that tradition under the Constitution of the United States.

The equity power was never intended to be used to grant broad remedies to entire social classes; rather, it was intended to provide particular relief to specific individuals in cases where the aggrieved party had suffered a clear and irreparable injury for which the law, by its generality,

121

could not provide a plain and adequate remedy. The invocation of the equity power by the Court in the school-desegregation cases has been little more than a sophistical means of cloaking its policymaking in the comfortable trappings of traditional judicial language. The result has been public policy, not equitable relief.

The Court has expanded its power beyond what its constitutional foundation can legitimately support. The cure for this constitutional usurpation is not to be found in any empty wish for judicial self-restraint; it is to be found in the proper workings of the scheme of separation of powers for which the Constitution provides. If the Court is to be restrained, it must be as the result of Congress's exercising (1) its constitutional powers to regulate the appellate equity jurisdiction of the Supreme Court and (2) its power to regulate the original jurisdiction and equity procedures in the inferior federal courts. It is necessary to recover two things: first, the older understanding of the problematic nature of equity in a nation based on a written constitution and dedicated to the rule of law; second, a stricter procedural distinction between law and equity.

Epilogue

John Stuart Mill   The disposition of mankind, whether as rulers or as
fellow citizens, to impose their own opinions and inclinations as a rule of conduct on others, is so energeti-
cally supported by some of the best and some of the
worst feelings incident to human nature, that it is hardly
ever kept under restraint by anything but want of power.

Toward a Recovery of the Past

Since the time of its creation—or at least since John Marshall became chief justice in 1801—the Supreme Court has never been immune to politics. Whether from the Jeffersonian Republicans, the Jacksonians, the Abolitionists, the Radical Republicans, the Progressives, or the New Dealers, each Court, throughout our history, has enjoyed the praise and suffered the blame of being "political" or "activist." Whatever the time and whatever the issue, the Supreme Court has always found itself in the thick of the debates that have animated American political life. The current controversy over the "egalitarian society," with all its equitable overtones, is no different. This is due in no slight measure to the Constitution itself, for nearly every issue in American politics comes ultimately to be measured by the standard of the Constitution. Constitutionality is the fundamental source of our political legitimacy. Hence the Supreme Court—an institution "peculiarly essential in a limited constitution"[1]—is eventually drawn into the fray and asked to exercise its judgment as the final arbiter of conflicting claims of constitutionality. The power of judgment wielded by the Court is awesome, so awesome, in fact, that the Founders saw fit to give it this power alone and to deny it the necessary tools of implementation. The Founders agreed with Montesquieu: "There is no liberty, if the power of judging be not separated from the legislative and executive powers."[2] Force

125

and will, the executive and legislative powers, respectively, were not intended to be components of judicial review.

Judicial review, though not explicitly provided for by the Constitution, was anticipated by the Founders and assumed to be inherent in the judicial power. The power of judicial review was understood to be an essentially negative power. As Alexander Hamilton succinctly put it, judicial review is "the right of the courts to pronounce legislative acts void because contrary to the Constitution."[3] The judiciary was designed as an "intermediate body between the people and the legislature in order, among other things, to keep the latter within the limits assigned to their authority." Hamilton went on:

> The interpretation of the laws is the proper and peculiar province of the courts. A constitution is in fact, and must be, regarded by the judges as fundamental law. It therefore belongs to them to ascertain its meaning as well as the meaning of any particular act proceeding from the legislative body. If there should happen to be an irreconcilable variance between the two, that which has the superior obligation and validity ought of course to be preferred; or in other words, the constitution ought to be preferred to the statute, the intention of the people to the intention of their agents.[4]

The courts, according to Hamilton, since they were intended to be the "bulwarks of a limited constitution," should possess the institutional force to resist "legislative encroachments." Should the courts ever be "disposed to exercise *will* instead of *judgment*, the consequence would equally be the substitution of their pleasure to that of the legislative body."[5] That is, they would be substituting their will for the will of the people; they would in essence be creating a will independent of society itself.[6] Judicial presumption of this kind was considered by the Founders to be intolerable, and provisions to check it were provided by the Constitution. As Hamilton observed:

> Particular misconstructions and contraventions of the will of the legislature may now and then happen; but they can never be so extensive as to amount to an inconvenience, or in any sensible degree to affect the order of the political system. This may be inferred with certainty from the general nature of the judicial power; from the objects to which it relates, from the manner in which it is exercised, from its comparative weakness, and from its total incapacity to support its usurpations by force. And the inference is greatly fortified by the consideration of the important constitutional check, which the power of instituting impeachments, in one part of the legislative body, and of determining upon them in the other, would give to that body upon the members of the judicial department.[7]

Beyond the most drastic constitutional check—impeachment—the legislature controlled the appellate jurisdiction of the Supreme Court, as well as the creation and implementation of all inferior tribunals. The judiciary could safely be entrusted to exercise the power of constitutional judgment because, on the basis of its power as defined by the Constitution, it would be unable to take "any active resolution whatever."[8] Should it be overwhelmed by a sense of its own self-righteousness and attempt to express its will rather than its judgment, Congress could safely bring it back within the republican fold.

Although the Court's critics may insist that judicial vetoes of legislative enactments are, in a very real sense, expressions of a judicial will, the power of judicial review still seems to fit comfortably with the original understanding of the judicial function. Certainly *pro*scriptive rather than *pre*scriptive judicial decrees were what were intended by those who drafted and ratified the Constitution. Until the *Brown* decisions in 1954–55, most judicial opinions took the form of prohibiting actions deemed unconstitutional rather than commanding actions thought necessary to attain the good life under the Constitution. The prescriptive decrees of *Brown* (II), *Green, Carter, Swann, Hills,* and *Milliken* (II) are clear examples of a new judicial view of the judicial function. They are, to be sure, the results of a new sociological understanding of the inherently positive "historic equitable remedial powers" (in contradistinction to the inherently negative power of judicial review) possessed by the federal judiciary. But this new notion of equity has been made possible only by a new and widely accepted judicial view of the Constitution itself.

I

The object of the Constitutional Convention in 1787, it was frequently asserted, was to draft a constitution "for future generations, and not merely for the peculiar circumstances of the moment";[9] the Founders hoped they had devised a Constitution that would "last forever" or, at the very least, one that would "last for ages."[10]

The Constitution was intended to be "paramount," "fundamental," and lasting in order to achieve a steady and just administration of the laws.[11] By being held above the law, the Constitution would contribute to the necessary political stability by drawing unto itself that "veneration which time bestows on everything."[12] Certainly the Founders entertained no utopian notions that they had written the last word in republican constitutions; they knew the necessity of allowing for future amendments. But they also understood that the process of changing the fundamental and paramount law not only must rest with the people but also must be so cumbersome that it would not be used for "light and transient causes."

They saw the danger in rendering the Constitution "too mutable."[13] The Constitution was left to posterity not merely to improve but to "improve and perpetuate,"[14] and the alteration of the Constitution to meet the unforeseen exigencies of the future was left to the people, not to their deputies alone.

This older view of the Constitution as paramount to the ordinary law and to the branches of the government has become undermined to a great degree by a new judicial view of the Constitution. This view is made up of two distinct but related lines of judicial logic. The first is that the opinions of the Supreme Court—constitutional law—have the same status as the Constitution itself; the second is that the Constitution is not bound by any particular political theory, is not permanent and fixed, but is instead free to move amoeba-like through history. Although this new view did not, perhaps, originate with the Warren Court, it received its clearest articulation there.

In *Cooper* v. *Aaron*—a case involving implementation of *Brown*—the Supreme Court elevated its opinions to the status of "supreme Law of the Land." In a line of judicial reasoning that may be described as tenuous, the Court insisted that it was only recalling "some basic constitutional propositions which are settled doctrine." First, the Court pointed out that "Article VI of the Constitution makes the Constitution 'the supreme Law of the Land.'" Then, citing John Marshall's opinion in *Marbury* v. *Madison,* the Court put forth its novel doctrine:

> This decision [*Marbury*] declared the basic principle that the federal judiciary is supreme in the exposition of the law of the Constitution, and that principle has ever since been respected by this Court and the Country as a permanent and indispensable feature of our constitutional system. It follows that the interpretation of the Fourteenth Amendment enunciated in this Court in the *Brown* case is the supreme law of the land. [At 18–19]

The Court in *Cooper* v. *Aaron* endeavored to obliterate the distinction between the Constitution and constitutional law; the two had never been explicitly considered to be synonymous. The Constitution was considered the supreme law in that it represented the public will. It was mutable, to be sure, but only by the intricate and lengthy process of formal amendment. Constitutional law, on the other hand, was not considered supreme law, because, being the mere product of interpretations of the supreme will of the people by agents of the people, it was susceptible of error. The justices of the Supreme Court were no more expected to be that "philosophical race of kings wished for by Plato"[15] than any other deputy of the people—representative, senator, or president.

The Constitution is more fundamental than constitutional law in the same sense that it is more fundamental than legislative enactments.[16] Constitutional law and legislative enactments are, and must be, more mutable than the Constitution. To assume that constitutional law is somehow by its nature an immutable part of the "supreme law of the land" is to conjure up frightening conclusions not only about the "derelicts of constitutional law"[17] (e.g., *Dred Scott* v. *Sandford*)[18] but, at a deeper level, about the necessity of maintaining certainty in the administration of a republican form of government. The Court, in *Cooper* v. *Aaron,* it seems, took too seriously Charles Evans Hughes's nonjudicial dictum that the "Constitution is what the judges say it is."[19]

This notion of the supremacy of judicial opinions was rendered even more problematical by the related line of the new constitutional logic. In *Harper* v. *Virginia Board of Elections* Mr. Justice Douglas, writing for the majority of a bitterly divided Court, insisted that:

> The Equal Protection Clause is not shackled to the political theory of a particular era. In determining what lines are unconstitutionally discriminatory, we have never been confined to historic notions of equality any more than we have restricted due process to a fixed catalogue of what was at a given time deemed to be the limits of fundamental rights. [At 669]

"Notions of what constitutes equal treatment for purposes of the Equal Protection Clause," Douglas emphasized, "*do* change."

Between these two lines of judicial logic—the alleged supremacy of Supreme Court opinions, and the notion that the meaning of the Constitution changes from one era to another—lies the fundamentally new judicial view of the Constitution, the idea of a "living Constitution." As Felix Frankfurter pointed out as early as 1937, the "people have been taught to believe that when the Supreme Court speaks it is not [the justices] who speak but the Constitution, whereas, of course, in so many vital cases, it is *they* who speak and *not* the Constitution.... And verily I believe," Frankfurter concluded, "that this is what the country needs most to understand."[20] The idea of a "living Constitution" is, in the words of Justice Black, "an attack not only on the great value of our Constitution itself, but also on the concept of a written constitution which is to survive through the years as originally written unless changed through the amending process which the Framers wisely provided."[21]

To try to instill an appreciation for the distinction between the Constitution and what the judges say it is in their opinions is no mean task. While one may argue against the view that many of its commands are "written in Delphic language,"[22] the Constitution is certainly not free of

129

"indeterminate language."[23] Nor is the application of the language of the Constitution a merely "mechanical process." But however indeterminate its language may be, and however much judgment may be necessary in applying its provisions, "there are large areas of clarity in constitutional language which could limit the operations of government by providing limits to the discretion of those who apply constitutional rules."[24] As Sotirios Barber has argued, in order to "restore somewhat the distinction between the Constitution and its judicial gloss," it is necessary to point out that a "coherent account of events in judicial history requires principles which transcend the cases themselves. . . . The meaning of the Constitution itself is one source of those principles, as are such other sources as the deeper intentions of the Framers and the needs of current generations."[25]

In order to evaluate fully the constitutional implications of the Court's new doctrine of "sociological" equity, it is important to recall the original intention of the Constitution and to reconsider the precedents and principles of equity jurisprudence. It is necessary as well to consider that the best interests of aggrieved social classes may be better served by preservation of the institutional equilibrium of an emphatically limited Constitution, dedicated to the rule of law, than by the transient opinions of judges, however noble their consciences or senses of "moral duty" may appear, at a given moment, to be.

II

The basic intention of the Framers, taking into account the permanent attributes of human nature, both its strengths and its weaknesses, was to create a government that could be safely administered by men over men. The end sought was a safe balance between governmental power and individual liberty or, as Madison explained in *The Federalist*, to combine "the requisite stability and energy in government with the inviolable attention due to liberty and the Republican form."[26] The Constitution was the magnificent product; it was understood to create an institutional arrangement for achieving the political principles of the Declaration of Independence and for securing the most hallowed of the Framers' objects, political liberty.[27] One of the most enduring of the threats to political liberty in a popular regime of which the Constitution took account was the problem of majority factions.[28] These were the "mortal diseases under which popular governments [had] everywhere perished."[29] Majority faction was seen as a problem of popular government because the form of the government itself could enable an "overbearing" majority to "sacrifice to its ruling passion or interest both the public good and the rights of other citizens."[30] To prevent such popular tyranny—or at least to hedge against it—the Framers sought to construct a political system laden with internal checks, such as separation of powers, representation, bicameralism, federalism, and "courts of judges holding their offices during good behavior."[31] An independent and vital judiciary was deemed a peculiarly essential "auxiliary precaution" under the limited constitution being drafted.[32] As Alexander Hamilton said in *Federalist*, No. 78:

> It is not with a view to infractions of the Constitution only that the independence of the judges may be an essential safeguard against the effects of occasional ill humors in the society. These sometimes extend no farther than to the injury of private rights of particular classes of citizens by unjust and partial laws. Here also the firmness of the judicial magistracy is of vast importance in mitigating the severity and confining the operation of such laws.[33]

The judicial power was created by the Constitution to "extend to all cases in law and equity" as a means of maintaining a constitutional equilibrium that would render governmental power safe for political liberty. Equity would be—in particular instances—an appropriate judicial power for restraining the operation and enforcement of any "unjust and partial laws." *De jure* racial discrimination is an example (to use James Madison's telling description) of public policy being decided not "according to the rules of justice and the rights of the minor party, but by the superior force of an interested and overbearing majority."[34]

In the *Brown* v. *Board of Education of Topeka, Kansas* cases, the Court would have been on firmer ground—both constitutionally and jurisprudentially—had it approached the "separate but equal" doctrine as an infringement of liberty rather than as a denial of equality. Without constructing the dubious doctrine of psychological equality which can be violated by a "feeling of inferiority," the Court could have reached the merits of the case by arguing that the Equal Protection Clause was intended to secure political liberty for Negroes and that the essence of political liberty is freedom to live one's life without the pressures of legally imposed burdens based solely on race. Such a view would have had considerably more support in the legislative history of the Fourteenth Amendment than the idea that the Amendment either intended or was simply conveniently silent on the idea of social equality for Negroes. Since it seems apparent that the Warren Court's predecessor, the Vinson Court, had been moving toward an abandonment of the "separate but equal" doctrine for some time, the Warren Court, in *Brown*, could have reversed the majority opinion in *Plessy* v. *Ferguson* without ever having to enter the uncertain realm of psychology and sociology.[35] Following the dissent of the elder John Marshall Harlan in *Plessy*, the Court, in *Brown*, could have invalidated the "separate but equal" doctrine as an unconstitutional infringement of liberty because it allowed the states to deny to a portion of their citizens, on the basis of "partial laws,"[36] the freedom to choose how to live their lives.

By reaching what it believed to be the psychological merits of the case in *Brown*, the Court lost sight of the problem of maintaining liberty for the individual. A "feeling of inferiority" became a problem not of the individual but of the entire race. Hence the Supreme Court moved toward a new understanding of equal protection of the laws dedicated to generating a feeling of social equality among all citizens rather than toward insuring the political liberty of the individual citizen.[37] The "historic equitable remedial powers" of the federal judiciary were then put into the service of this new understanding of equality and used in the judicial attempt to achieve a feeling of equality among the citizens. For the first time, equity was to be used explicitly for furthering a particular political goal rather than as a judicial means of confining unjust and partial laws. The result has been the new "sociological" understanding of equitable relief. From what was thought at the Founding to offer relief to individuals from "hard bargains" has come the asserted judicial power power to draw the line between governmental powers and the rights of "discrete and insular minorities" and to create remedies for past encroachments against whole classes of people. Such broad decrees of relief, "fashioned and effectuated" on the basis of "equitable principles," are in essence judicially created social policies. The result has been judicial activism with a vengeance.

What is most significant about judicial activism is not that the judiciary is behaving in an unexpected manner. The judges are men and are behaving as we must expect all men in positions of such power to behave. All power—judicial as well as legislative and executive—is of an encroaching nature. Left to themselves, all political men will go as far as they can in pursuit of their view of the political good. What is most significant is, then, not judicial usurpation of power but congressional abdication of it. Judicial activism is the result of Congress's failing to exercise its constitutional prerogatives over matters of jurisdiction and procedure and of its specifically increasing the scope of equitable relief by giving the courts the power to enforce particular statutes through their equitable powers.[38]

III

The Constitution does not leave republican safety and the security of political liberty to good intentions. It creates a detailed scheme of separation of powers, with enough "partial agency" left among the three branches to insure a safe separation. It seeks to supply "by opposite and rival interests, the defect of better motives." As Madison explained it in *Federalist*, No. 51:

> [T]he great security against a gradual concentration of the several powers in the same department, consists in giving to those who administer each department, the necessary constitutional means, and personal motives, to resist encroachments of the others. The provision for defense must in this, as in all other cases, be made commensurate to the danger of attack. Ambition must be made to counteract ambition. The interest of the man must be connected with the constitutional rights of the place.[39]

Although it was the legislative power the Founders feared most, they were not blind to the possibility that each department might be inclined to extend its authority beyond the limits safely assigned to it. The judiciary was intended "from the nature of its functions" to be the branch "least dangerous to the political rights of the Constitution." The liberty of the people would be safe from judicial power only "so long as the judiciary remains truly distinct from both the legislative and executive."[40] The formulation of policy is a distinctly legislative function; a judiciary that undertakes to make such choices infringes upon the legislative power. To violate the separation of powers, an institutional collusion is not required; the violation occurs when any of the branches of the government proceeds to exercise the *power* which was assigned by the Constitution to one of the coordinate branches.

Recognizing that such judicial usurpations could take place, the Framers made provisions to check it. Most obviously, the executive could refuse to enforce the decisions of the Court, or the legislature could initiate impeachment proceedings. On a more practical level, the Constitution provides for a more appropriate pressure on a recalcitrant Court.[41] On the basis of the Constitution, Congress possesses the power to regulate the appellate jurisdiction of the Supreme Court as well as the power to constitute and regulate all inferior tribunals. In all the areas that the Court has reached under the new "sociological" equity, the equity power can be regulated and restricted by Congress in two ways: (1) by the rules of civil procedure and (2) by limiting the use of the power in the particular statutes it enacts.

There seems to be sufficient evidence to support a call for a return to the mode of civil procedure in which law and equity are procedurally distinct. Such a course would recover the older understanding of the problematical nature of equity jurisprudence and would preclude judges, in the telling language of the "Federal Farmer," from switching from their shoes of law to their shoes of equity whenever they found that the law restrained them. The most apparent objection to such a recovery of the old method of procedure would be the one that led to its demise in the first place. The rigid procedural distinction between law and equity is cumbersome—and slow. To borrow, out of context, the language of Chief Justice Burger, a separated system of pleadings "may be administratively awkward, inconvenient, and even bizarre in some situations and may impose burdens on some." But "awkwardness and inconvenience" cannot be sufficient to deny an enforcement of the Constitution's provisions for a separation of the powers of government.

Republican safety and political liberty are of a more elevated status under the Constitution than a concern for efficiency in the administration of the government. To counter the resistance of those who would deny the necessity of recovering the past to the extent of separating equity from law, we could find no better authority, nor one more appropriate, than the greatest American student of equity jurisprudence, Joseph Story:

> If there be any truth, which a large survey of human experience justifies us in asserting, it is, that, in proportion as a government is free, it must be complicated.[42]

IV

There is an intimate connection between judicial power and public opinion. Not only does the Court, as a "republican schoolmaster," help shape public opinion, but it also usually comes, in turn, to be supported by the opinion it has shaped. Judicial opinions tend to be woven into the fabric of the American political consciousness to such a degree that they are taken for granted. This is the result of the tendency in American politics—and, on the whole, it is a commendable tendency—to defer to the "moral force" of the judiciary. What is undesirable about this popular deference is that too often it precludes the necessary public awareness that the judiciary is, fundamentally, a political institution and, as such, is susceptible of error. That the judiciary may be exercising its powers in an unhealthy or unconstitutional way is usually a matter only whispered about in scholarly closets. On the whole, the people believe the Court to be apolitical and beyond reproach, and that belief is a massive, if not insurmountable, obstacle to Congress's exercising any meaningful control over the judicial power. Felix Frankfurter was correct when he argued that "exposure of the Court's abuse of its powers will bring about a shift in the Court's viewpoint."[43] It is certainly the "prime task of scholarship . . . to heighten public awareness that the court has been overleaping its bounds."[44] But the task is not limited to legal scholarship; it is also the primary task of political leadership.

In the areas reached under the Court's equity powers, the Court has cultivated a strong constituency. Most assuredly, it would be "utterly unrealistic and probably impossible to undo the past" in the face of increased expectations generated by the Court's actions.[45] But undoing the past is not as important as preparing for the future. The expanded use of the equitable remedial powers can be curtailed without disturbing the things it has been used to achieve in the past. The inability to correct past abuses need not prevent us from endeavoring to prevent future ones.

One of the great strengths of the American political order is the animating belief that in certain instances political leaders must cut against the grain of popular opinion in order best to serve the *interests* of the people when these interests are at variance with their *inclinations*.[46] On such occasions it is necessary to persuade—or at least attempt to persuade—the people of the rightness of an alternate view. The first step in righting our current judicial wrongs is to muster all possible rhetorical force against the prevalent view and to educate public opinion.

Any attempt to reverse the trend toward a seemingly limitless equitable remedial power of the judiciary will fly in the face of a good many political passions, but, by a carefully calculated appeal to reason, such passions can be calmed. The key is to show two things. First, the same ends—ends generally supported by "most decent instincts"[47]—can be achieved through different, more legitimate means—means less arbitrary and capricious than unfettered judicial opinion. Second, and more important, judicial opinion is not gospel; it may be questioned, and it may be challenged. In brief, the task is to teach our generation the lesson Abraham Lincoln, in the shadow of *Dred Scott*, attempted to teach his:

> [that] if the policy of government, upon vital questions affecting the whole people, is to be irrevocably fixed by decisions of the Supreme Court, the instant they are made, in ordinary litigation between parties, in personal actions, the people will have ceased to be their own rulers, having, to that extent, practically resigned their government, into the hands of that eminent tribunal.[48]

Notes

Introduction

1. See, especially, Henry J. Abraham, *Freedom and the Court* 3d ed. (New York: Oxford University Press, 1977), pp. 415–40; Alexander M. Bickel, *The Supreme Court and the Idea of Progress* (New York: Harper & Row, 1970); Raoul Berger, *Government by Judiciary* (Cambridge, Mass.: Harvard University Press, 1977); Donald L. Horowitz, *The Courts and Social Policy* (Washington, D.C.: The Brookings Institution, 1977); Lino Graglia, *Disaster by Decree* (Ithaca: Cornell University Press, 1976); Nathan Glazer, *Affirmative Discrimination* (New York: Basic Books, 1975); Jethro K. Lieberman, *The Litigious Society* (New York: Basic Books 1981); and the various essays in Gary L. McDowell, ed., *Taking the Constitution Seriously* (Dubuque: Kendall-Hunt, 1981).

2. *The Federalist,* No. 80, in Jacob Cooke, ed., *The Federalist* (Middletown, Conn.: Wesleyan University Press, 1961), p. 539. All references are to this edition, hereafter cited as *Federalist*.

3. *Federalist,* No. 78, p. 528.

4. Unless otherwise indicated, all translations of classical authors are from the Loeb Classical Library editions, listed in the Bibliography.

5. *Rees v. Watertown,* 19 Wallace 107, 121 (1873).

6. Letter XI, January 31, 1788, in Herbert J. Storing, ed., *The Complete Anti-Federalist,* 7 vols. (Chicago: University of Chicago Press, 1981), 2.9.137, and 2.9.144. All references to the Anti-Federalists are to this edition, hereafter cited as *Storing.* The first number denotes the volume, the second the position of the essay or series within that volume, and the third the paragraph.

7. Letter XV, January 18, 1788, in *Storing,* 2.8.185, 2.8.195; and Letter IV, October 12, 1787, 2.8.42.

8. 2 Dallas 414 (1792).

9. Benjamin N. Cardozo, *The Nature of the Judicial Process* (New Haven: Yale University Press, 1921), p. 51.

10. Horowitz, *The Courts and Social Policy*, p. 7.

11. Max Farrand, ed., *The Records of the Federal Convention*, 4 vols. (New Haven: Yale University Press, 1937), 2:73. All references are to this edition, hereafter cited as *Farrand*.

12. *Federalist*, No. 49, p. 341.

13. The new use of the equitable remedial powers has been strangely slighted in two recent and important books on the nature of the judicial process: John Hart Ely, *Democracy and Distrust* (Cambridge, Mass.: Harvard University Press, 1980), and Jesse Choper, *Judicial Review and the National Political Process* (Chicago: University of Chicago Press, 1980). The new equity has had at least one formidable advocate, however. Owen M. Fiss, in *The Civil Rights Injunction* (Bloomington: Indiana University Press, 1978), applauds what he considers to be the "triumph of *Brown*" and the creative use by the Court of the injunction. In particular, he ardently defends judicial relief in the form of the *reparative* injunction, "which compels the defendant to engage in a course of action that seeks to correct the effects of a past wrong," and the *structural* injunction, "which seeks to effectuate the reorganization of an ongoing social institution" (p. 7). Fiss's celebration of the civil rights injunction, however, becomes intelligible only if one abandons the received wisdom of the tradition of equity jurisprudence, which holds the injunction to be a truly "extraordinary" power, one that should of necessity be subordinated in the hierarchy of judicial remedies. For Fiss, the end sought seems to justify the means chosen: "Form follows substance" (p. 15). As a result, he is willing to grant that it is legitimate for the courts "to create the terms of their own legitimacy" (p. 95). As Fiss's analysis shows, the unfettering of injunctive relief from the principles and precedents that formerly chained it down leads inevitably to the enhancement of judicial policymaking: "The impact of *Brown* on our remedial jurisprudence—giving a primacy to the injunction—was not confined to school desegregation. It also extended to civil rights cases in general, and beyond civil rights to litigation involving electoral apportionment, mental hospitals, prisons, trade practices, and the environment" (p. 4). See also Abram Chayes, "The Role of the Judge in Public Law Litigation," *Harvard Law Review* 89 (1976):1281. Chayes's analysis goes beyond, but does include, a discussion of what he terms the "triumph of equity." A thoughtful response to Chayes is William Kristol's "The American Judicial Power and the American Regime" (Ph.D. diss., Harvard University, 1979).

Chapter One

1. See, for example, Thucydides, *History of the Peloponnesian War* 3. 37–40; Plato, *The Laws* 757d–e, 736d–e, 875c; Plato, *The Statesman* 294a.

2. Max Hamburger, *Morals and Law: The Growth of Aristotle's Legal Theory* (New York: Biblo & Tannen, 1965), p. 96.

3. Ibid.

4. It is necessary to keep in mind the nature of the Athenian courts and judges. See Appendix II in *The Politics of Aristotle*, trans. Ernest Barker (Oxford: Oxford University Press, 1946), p. 373, n. 3.

5. Ibid.

6. Henry Sumner Maine, *Ancient Law*, 2d ed. (London: John Murray, 1863), pp. 58–59.

7. Sir Frederick Pollock, *Essays in the Law* (London: Macmillan, 1922), p. 181. This collection contains a particularly good essay entitled "The Transformation of Equity."

8. Maine, *Ancient Law*, pp. 62–66.

9. See ibid., pp. 68–72; Pollock, *Essays in the Law*, pp. 181–95; and Charles S. Brice, "Roman Aequitas and English Equity," *Georgetown Law Journal* 2 (1913): 16.

10. Henry Adams, "The Anglo-Saxon Courts of Law," in *Essays in Anglo-Saxon Law* (Boston: Little, Brown, 1876).

11. Thomas Cooper, ed., *The Institutes of Justinian*, trans. George Harris (Philadelphia: P. Byrne, 1812), p. 1.

12. Ranulph de Glanville, *De Legibus et Consuetudinibus Regni Angliae*, ed. G. D. G. Hall (London: Thomas Nelson, 1965), p. 1.

13. Henrici de Bracton, *De Legibus et Consuetudinibus Angliae*, ed. Travers Twiss, 4 vols. (London: Longman, 1878), 1:3.

14. Compare, for example, the *Institutes*, 1. 1. 140 and 3. 1. 9 with Glanville's *De Legibus*, 7. 1–2.

15. See Cicero, *Ad Herennium*, 2. 13. 20, note d.

16. Bracton, *De Legibus*, 1:20–21.

17. Ibid., 1:19–25, 98, 187.

18. *Institutes*, 1. 1. 40; 3. 1. 9; Glanville, *De Legibus*, 7. 1–2; Bracton, *De Legibus*, 1:140, 314.

19. Christopher St. Germain, *Dialogues between a Doctor of Divinity and a Student in the Laws of England*, ed. William Muchall (Cincinnati: Robert Clarke, 1874).

20. Ibid., p. 44.

21. Ibid., pp. 44–45.

22. Ibid.

23. Pollock, *Essays in the Law*, pp. 192–93.

24. Ibid., p. 193.

25. George Burton Adams, "The Origins of English Equity," *Columbia Law Review* 16 (1916): 87. This essay is reprinted in Edward D. Re, *Selected Essays in Equity* (New York: Oceana, 1966), p. 5. Pagination cited is that of the Re volume.

26. See Adams, "The Origins of English Equity," p. 3; Henry J. Abraham, *The Judicial Process*, 4th ed. (New York: Oxford University Press, 1980), pp. 14–15; and Joseph Parkes, *A History of the Court of Chancery* (London: Longman, 1828).

27. Pollock, *Essays in the Law*, p. 187.

28. Abraham, *The Judicial Process*, p. 15.

29. Ibid., pp. 8–14; see also Theodore F. T. Plucknett, *A Concise History of the Common Law*, 5th ed. (Boston: Little, Brown, 1956).

30. Edward S. Corwin, *The "Higher Law" Background of American Constitutional Law* (Ithaca: Cornell University Press, 1955), p. 46.

31. Ibid., p. 45, n. 11.

32. Ibid., p. 42.

33. *Proclamations*, 12 Co. 74, 76 (1611), as cited in Corwin, p. 43. Bracton's words were: "The King himself ought not to be subject to man, but subject to God and to the Law, for the law makes the king. Let the king then attribute to the law what the law attributes to him, namely, dominion and power, for there is no king where the will and not the law has dominion" (*De Legibus*, 1. 5b).

34. *Prohibitions del Roy*, 7 Co. 63–65 (1609), as cited by Corwin, pp. 38–39.

35. Sir Edward Coke, *The First Part of the Institutes of the Laws of England*, ed. Charles Butler, 2 vols. (Philadelphia: Robert M. Small, 1853), vol. 1, sec. 21.

36. See D. Caulfield Heron, *An Introduction to the History of Jurisprudence* (London: John Parker, 1860), pp. 347–79.

37. Joseph Cropsey, Introduction to his edition of Thomas Hobbes, *A Dialogue between a Philosopher and a Student of the Common Laws of England* (Chicago: University of Chicago Press, 1971), p. 14.

38. Thomas Hobbes, *Leviathan* (Oxford: Oxford University Press, 1909), p. 119.

39. Ibid., p. 217.

40. Ibid., p. 207.

41. Hobbes, *Dialogue*, p. 54.

42. Ibid., pp. 70, 94–95.

43. Ibid., p. 97.

44. Ibid., p. 98.

45. Henry Home, Lord Kames, *Principles of Equity*, 2d ed. (Edinburgh: Bell & Bradfute, 1825).

46. Ibid., p. 8.

47. Ibid., p. 10. For the best discussion of the differences between antiquity and modernity, see Leo Strauss, *Natural Right and History* (Chicago: University of Chicago Press, 1953).

48. Ibid., p. 13.

49. Ibid., pp. 14, 13.

50. Morton J. Horwitz, *The Transformation of American Law: 1780–1860* (Cambridge, Mass.: Harvard University Press, 1977), p. 265.

51. William Blackstone, *Commentaries on the Laws of England*, 15th ed., 4 vols. (London: A. Strahan, 1809).

52. Ibid., 3:429.

53. Ibid., p. 433.

54. Ibid., p. 436.

55. Ibid., p. 440.

56. Ibid.

57. Ibid., p. 441.

58. John Taylor, *Elements of the Civil Law*, 4th ed. (London: S. Sweet, 1828).

59. Henry Ballow, *A Treatise of Equity*, ed. John Fonblanque, 2 vols. (Philadelphia: A. Small, 1820).

Chapter Two

1. Gordon S. Wood, *The Creation of the American Republic: 1776–1787* (Chapel Hill: University of North Carolina Press, 1969), p. 266. See also Corwin, *The "Higher Law" Background*.

2. Wood, *Creation of the American Republic*, pp. 296–97.

3. Governor Henry Moore of New York, as quoted by Irving Mark, *Agrarian Conflicts in Colonial New York: 1711–1775* (New York: Friedman, 1940), p. 77. I am indebted in this instance, as in a great many others, to the superb research of Gordon Wood as presented in his *The Creation of the American Republic*.

4. Julius Goebel, Jr., *History of the Supreme Court of the United States: Antecedents and Beginnings to 1801*, vol. 1 of the Oliver Wendell Holmes Devise (New York: Macmillan, 1971), p. 7, n. 8; hereafter cited as Goebel, *History*. See also Wood, *Creation of the American Republic*, p. 298.

5. Trevor Colburn, ed., "Pennsylvania Farmer," *Pennsylvania Magazine of History and Biography* 86 (1962): 450–51.

6. James Otis had proclaimed as early as 1761 that any "Act against Natural Equity is void" and must be passed into disuse by the courts. See Josiah Quincy, Jr., *Reports of Cases Signed and Adjudged in the Superior Court of Judicature of . . . Massachusetts Bay . . . 1761–1772* (Boston, 1865), pp. 471–74.

7. William Drayton, in a speech before the General Assembly of South Carolina, January 20, 1778, in Hezekiah Niles, ed., *Principles and Acts of the Revolution in America* (New York, 1876), p. 359.

8. Thomas Jefferson to Edmund Pendleton, August 26, 1776, in Julian Boyd, ed., *The Papers of Thomas Jefferson* (Princeton: Princeton University Press, 1950——), vol. 1, pp. 503, 505.

9. Thomas Jefferson, "A Summary View of the Rights of British America," ibid., pp. 121, 134.

10. As quoted by Wood, *Creation of the American Republic*, p. 456.

11. *Pennsylvania Packet*, October 10, 1787, in *Pennsylvania and the Federal Constitution, 1787–1788*, ed. John Bach McMaster and Frederick D. Stone, 2 vols. (New York: Da Capo, 1970), 1:153. This edition is an unabridged republication of the first edition, published in Philadelphia in 1888.

12. *Farrand*, 2:428.

13. Julius Goebel, Jr., ed., *The Law Practice of Alexander Hamilton: Documents and Commentary*, 2 vols. (New York: Columbia University Press, 1964), 1:172. Hereafter cited as *Law Practice*.

14. Ibid., p. 181.

15. Ibid., p. 167.

16. The *Rutgers* case and its progeny are covered in great detail in Goebel, *Law Practice*, 1:282–543, and my account of the facts of the case follows that of Goebel in his commentary.

17. Ibid., pp. 339, 338.

18. Ibid., p. 391.

19. Ibid., pp. 415–17.

20. *Federalist,* No. 78, p. 525.

21. Ibid., p. 528.

22. *Federalist,* No. 83, p. 560.

23. Ibid., pp. 568–70.

24. *Federalist,* No. 80, pp. 539–40.

25. Ibid., p. 538.

26. *Federalist,* No. 83, p. 569.

27. Ibid.

28. *Federalist,* No. 37, p. 236.

29. *Federalist,* No. 80, p. 538.

30. Robert G. McCloskey, ed., *The Works of James Wilson,* 2 vols. (Cambridge, Mass.: Harvard University Press, 1967), 1:68, 2:707.

31. Ibid., 2:486.

32. Ibid., p. 479.

33. Ibid., p. 486.

34. Ibid., pp. 478–79.

35. James Wilson's notes of the Pennsylvania ratifying debate in McMaster and Stone, eds., *Pennsylvania and the Federal Constitution,* 2:779.

36. Jonathan Elliot, ed., *The Debates in the Several State Conventions on the Adoption of the Federal Constitution,* 5 vols. (Philadelphia: J. B. Lippincott, 1896), 3:521.

37. Ibid., p. 524.

38. Letter XI of January 31, 1788, in *Storing,* 2.9.137.

39. Ibid.

40. Ibid.

41. Letter XII of February 7, 1788, in *Storing,* 2.9.145.

42. Letter III of October 10, 1787, in *Storing,* 2.8.185.

43. Goebel, *History,* p. 459.

44. *The Journal of William Maclay,* ed. E. S. Maclay (New York: Boni, 1927), p. 29. Hereafter cited as *Journal.* See also Seth Ames, ed., *Works of Fisher Ames,* 2 vols. (Boston: Little, Brown, 1854), 1:61, 64.

45. Goebel, *History,* p. 471.

46. Ibid., p. 480.

47. Maclay, *Journal,* p. 92.

48. Goebel, *History,* p. 484.

49. Maclay, *Journal,* p. 104.

50. *Senate Journal,* 1st sess., p. 63.

51. *Senate Journal,* 1st sess., 2d Cong., p. 119.

52. As cited by Goebel, *History,* p. 545, n. 164.

53. *The Public Statutes at Large of the United States of America, from . . . 1789 to 1845,* ed. Richard Peters, published by authority of Congress, 5 vols. (Boston: Little, Brown, 1850), 1:275.

54. 2 Dallas 414 (1792). See also Goebel, *History,* p. 547, n. 178.

Chapter Three

1. Strauss, *Natural Right and History*. See also Leo Strauss, *The Political Philosophy of Hobbes* (Chicago: University of Chicago Press, 1936).

2. Strauss, *Natural Right and History*, p. 180.

3. Hobbes's political philosophy is presented in three books, *The Elements of Law* (1640), *De Cive* (1642), and *Leviathan* (1651). For an interesting analysis of Hobbes's conception of fear in the scheme of politics see Richard Schlatter's Introduction to his *Hobbes's Thucydides* (New Brunswick, N.J.: Rutgers University Press, 1975).

4. An excellent analysis of Wilson's political thought, more broadly considered, is Ralph A. Rossum, "The Federal Pyramid: The Political Thought of James Wilson" (Ph.D. diss., University of Chicago, 1973).

5. McCloskey, ed., *The Works of James Wilson*, 1:126–47, 334–68.

6. Ibid., p. 130.

7. Ibid., p. 132.

8. Ibid., p. 133.

9. Ibid., p. 135.

10. Ibid., p. 137.

11. Ibid.

12. Ibid., p. 356.

13. Ibid., p. 353.

14. Ibid., p. 120.

15. Ibid., p. 122.

16. Ibid.

17. Ibid., p. 353.

18. Horwitz, *Transformation of American Law*, p. 22.

19. Ibid., p. 30.

20. Ibid., p. 2.

21. See James Morton Smith, *Freedom's Fetters* (Ithaca: Cornell University Press, 1956), and Richard E. Ellis, *The Jeffersonian Crisis* (New York: Oxford University Press, 1971).

22. Boyd, ed., *Papers of Thomas Jefferson*, 1:505.

23. Thomas Jefferson to Wilson C. Nicholas, September 5, 1779, in Paul Leicester Ford, ed., *The Writings of Thomas Jefferson*, 10 vols. (New York: Putnam's, 1896), 7:389.

24. *Farrand*, 2:316.

25. Ibid., pp. 316, 312.

26. Ibid., p. 637.

27. James Madison to George Washington, October 18, 1787, in Robert A. Rutland and Charles F. Hobson, eds., *The Papers of James Madison* (Chicago: University of Chicago Press, 1977), 10:196.

28. *Annals*, 5th Cong., 2d sess., pp. 2145–57. See also Smith, *Freedom's Fetters*, pp. 131–55.

29. *Annals*, 5th Cong., 2d sess., pp. 2157–59.

30. See Walter Berns, *The First Amendment and the Future of American Democracy* (New York: Basic Books, 1976), pp. 80–146.

31. Ford, ed., *Writings of Thomas Jefferson,* 7:383.
32. Edmund Randolph, "Notes on the Common Law," Library of Congress.
33. Ford, ed., *Writings of Thomas Jefferson,* 7:384.
34. Ibid.
35. Thomas Jefferson to Gideon Granger, August 13, 1800, ibid., p. 450.
36. James Madison to George Washington, April 16, 1787, in Rutland and Rachal, eds., *Papers of James Madison,* 9:382.
37. Marvin Meyers, ed., *The Mind of the Founder: Sources of the Political Thought of James Madison* (Indianapolis: Bobbs-Merrill, 1973), p. 318.
38. Ibid., p. 320.
39. Ibid., p. 324.
40. Ibid., p. 325.
41. Charles Warren, *A History of the American Bar* (Boston: Little, Brown, 1911), p. 508.
42. Daniel Raymond, "Law Reform in Regard to Real Estate," *Western Law Journal* 3 (1846): 385, as cited in Carl B. Swisher, *History of the Supreme Court of the United States: The Taney Period, 1836–64,* vol. 5 of the Oliver Wendell Holmes Devise (New York: Macmillan, 1974), p. 340. Hereafter cited as *The Taney Period.*
43. Ibid., p. 342. See Gertrude Himmelfarb, *On Liberty and Liberalism* (New York: Knopf, 1974), pp. 4–22 and passim.
44. Arthur James Johns, "On the Legal Arguments Urged in England for a Continuation of the Separation of the Law and Equity Jurisdictions," *American Jurist* 20 (1838): 115.
45. Swisher, *The Taney Period,* p. 341.
46. Horwitz, *Transformation of American Law,* p. 257.
47. John Milton Goodenow, *Historical Sketches of the Principles and Maxims of American Jurisprudence* (Steubenville, Ohio: James Wilson, 1819).
48. Ibid., p. 3.
49. Ibid., p. 4.
50. Ibid.
51. Ibid., p. 33.
52. Ibid., pp. 36–37.
53. Ibid., p. 38.
54. Peter S. DuPonceau, *A Dissertation on the Nature and Extent of the Jurisdiction of the Courts of the United States* (Philadelphia: Abraham Small, 1924).
55. James Madison to Peter DuPonceau, August 14, 1824, in the Madison Papers, Library of Congress. A fragment of this letter is reprinted in *Farrand,* 4:85.
56. DuPonceau, *Dissertation,* p. viii.
57. Ibid., p. x.
58. Ibid., p. xiii.
59. Ibid., p. xv.
60. Ibid., p. 91.
61. Peter DuPonceau to James Madison, September 13, 1824, in the Madison Papers, Library of Congress.

62. Ibid.

63. DuPonceau, *Dissertation*, p. xxv.

64. Ibid., p. 131.

65. Ibid., p. 127.

66. Ibid., p. 131.

67. James Kent, *Commentaries on American Law*, 4 vols. (New York: O. Halsted, 1826).

68. As quoted by Lawrence M. Friedman, *A History of American Law* (New York: Simon & Schuster, 1973), p. 288.

69. Kent, *Commentaries*, 1:321.

70. Ibid., pp. 321–22.

71. Ibid., p. 465.

72. Ibid., p. 440.

73. Ibid.

74. James Gould, *A Treatise on the Principles of Pleading* (Boston: Lilly & Wait, 1832), p. viii.

75. Ibid., p. vii.

76. Ibid., p. ix.

77. Francis Hilliard, *The Elements of Law* (Boston: Hilliard, Gray, 1835), p. 8.

78. Ibid., p. v.

79. Ibid., p. vi.

80. Joseph Story, *Commentaries on Equity Jurisprudence* 2 vols. (Boston: Little, Brown, 1836), 1:8.

Chapter Four

1. Thomas Jefferson to Albert Gallatin, September 27, 1810, in *The Writings of Thomas Jefferson*, Library Edition, 20 vols. (New York, 1903), 12:429.

2. Thomas Jefferson to James Madison, October 15, 1810, in Ford, ed., *Writings of Thomas Jefferson*, 9:282.

3. See James P. McClellan, *Joseph Story and the American Constitution* (Norman: University of Oklahoma Press, 1971), pp. 39–45, and Gerald T. Dunne, *Joseph Story and the Rise of the Supreme Court* (New York: Simon & Schuster, 1970).

4. McClellan, *Joseph Story and the American Constitution*, p. 43.

5. Joseph Story, "Literary Tendencies of the Times," in *The Miscellaneous Writings of Joseph Story*, ed. W. W. Story (Boston: Little, Brown, 1852), pp. 747–48. Hereafter cited as *Misc. Writings*.

6. Story, "Characteristics of the Age," *Misc. Writings*, p. 359.

7. Joseph Story to Richard Peters, December 17, 1832, in *The Life and Letters of Joseph Story*, ed. W. W. Story, 2 vols. (Boston: Little, Brown, 1851), 2:112. Hereafter cited as *Life and Letters*.

8. Joseph Story to Mr. Justice McLean, May 10, 1837, ibid., 2:273.

9. Joseph Story to the Rev. John Brazer, November 10, 1836, ibid., p. 240.

10. Story, "Chancery Jurisdiction," *Misc. Writings*, p. 167.

11. Story, "The Progress of Jurisprudence," ibid., p. 223.

12. Story, "The Value and Importance of Legal Studies" and "The Progress of Jurisprudence," ibid., pp. 540, 205.
13. Story, "The Progress of Jurisprudence," ibid., p. 202.
14. Ibid., p. 234.
15. Joseph Story to the Rev. John Brazer, November 10, 1836, *Life and Letters,* 2:240.
16. Story, "The Progress of Jurisprudence," *Misc. Writings,* pp. 203–5, 234, 205.
17. Joseph Story, *Commentaries on Equity Jurisprudence,* 3d ed., 2 vols. (Boston: Little, Brown, 1842), 1:1–2.
18. Ibid.
19. Ibid., p. 4.
20. Ibid., p. 7.
21. Joseph Story, "Law, Legislation, and Codes," *Encyclopedia Americana* (1831), 7:360, and *Commentaries on Equity Jurisprudence,* 1:9. Story's *Encyclopedia Americana* articles have been reprinted in McClellan, *Joseph Story and the American Constitution,* and all of my references are to the pagination of the McClellan volume.
22. Story, *Commentaries on Equity Jurisprudence,* 1:8.
23. Ibid., pp. 14–16. See *Cowper* v. *Cowper,* 2 P. Will. 753.
24. Story, *Commentaries on Equity Jurisprudence,* 1:16.
25. Ibid., p. 19.
26. Ibid., p. 21.
27. Ibid., p. 26.
28. Gerald T. Dunne, ed., "Joseph Story's First Writing on Equity," *American Journal of Legal History* 14 (1970): 79.
29. Story, *Commentaries on Equity Jurisprudence,* 1:26.
30. Dunne, ed., "Joseph Story's First Writing on Equity," p. 79.
31. Story, *Commentaries on Equity Jurisprudence,* 1:27.
32. Ibid.
33. Ibid., p. 30. See also Blackstone, *Commentaries on the Laws of England,* 1:92.
34. Story, *Commentaries on Equity Jurisprudence,* 1:32–33.
35. Story, "The Value and Importance of Legal Studies," *Misc. Writings,* p. 524.
36. Ibid., pp. 535, 506.
37. Dunne, ed., "Joseph Story's First Writing on Equity," p. 79.
38. Story, *Commentaries on Equity Jurisprudence,* 1:33.
39. Ibid., p. 35.
40. Story, "Chancery Jurisdiction," *Misc. Writings,* p. 169.
41. Ibid., pp. 169, 172.
42. See Letter XI of "Brutus" of January 31, 1788, and Letter III of "The Federal Farmer" of October 10, 1787, respectively, in *Storing,* 2.9.137 and 2.8.185; see also chap. 2, above.
43. Story, "Chancery Jurisdiction," *Misc. Writings,* pp. 170–71.

44. Joseph Story, *Commentaries on Equity Pleadings,* 3d ed. (Boston: Little, Brown, 1844), p. ix.
45. Story, "The Progress of Jurisprudence," *Misc. Writings,* p. 232.
46. Ibid., pp. 232, 233.
47. Joseph Story to James Kent, October 27, 1832, *Life and Letters,* 2:109.
48. Joseph Story, "A Eulogy of Chief Justice Parker of the Supreme Court of Massachusetts" (1831), *Life and Letters,* 2:75.
49. Story, "The Value and Importance of Legal Studies," *Misc. Writings,* p. 515.
50. Story, "Law, Legislation, and Codes," *Encyclopedia Americana,* p. 369.
51. Ibid., p. 365. See also Story, "Course of Legal Study," *Misc. Writings,* p. 70.
52. Story, "Law, Legislation, and Codes," *Encyclopedia Americana,* p. 350.
53. Ibid., p. 365.
54. Story, "Course of Legal Study," *Misc. Writings,* p. 70.
55. Ibid., p. 66.
56. Story, "Chancery Jurisdiction," *Misc. Writings,* pp. 166–67.
57. Story, "Codification and the Common Law," *Misc. Writings,* p. 702, and "The Value and Importance of Legal Studies," *Misc. Writings,* p. 526.
58. "The Value and Importance of Legal Studies," ibid., p. 504.
59. Story, "Course of Legal Study," *Misc. Writings,* p. 76.
60. Story, "Chancery Jurisdiction," ibid., p. 167.
61. Story, "Law, Legislation, and Codes," *Encyclopedia Americana,* pp. 359, 363.

Chapter Five

1. Alison Reppy, "The Field Codification Concept," in Alison Reppy, ed., *David Dudley Field: Centenary Essays* (New York: New York University School of Law, 1949), pp. 51–52. Hereafter cited as *Centenary Essays.*
2. Swisher, *The Taney Period,* pp. 347–48.
3. Henry M. Field, *The Life of David Dudley Field* (New York: Scribner's, 1898), pp. 42–43.
4. Reppy, "The Field Codification Concept," p. 30.
5. Swisher, *The Taney Period,* p. 348; see also H. M. Field, *Life of David Dudley Field,* pp. 44–45, and David Dudley Field, "Law Reform—State and International," in *Speeches, Arguments, and Miscellaneous Papers of David Dudley Field,* ed. A. P. Strague, 3 vols. (New York: Appleton, 1884–90), 1:219–583.
6. William D. Mitchell, "The Federal Rules of Civil Procedure," in Reppy, ed., *Centenary Essays,* p. 73.
7. Field, *Life of David Dudley Field,* p. 261.
8. Reppy, "The Field Codification Concept," p. 50.
9. Ibid., p. 30.
10. Ibid., pp. 31–32.
11. Field, *Life of David Dudley Field,* p. 47.

12. Reppy, "The Field Codification Concept," p. 32.

13. New York Laws, 1847, 744, as cited ibid., p. 33.

14. Field, *Life of David Dudley Field*, p. 49.

15. New York Laws, 1848 c. 379.

16. Friedman, *History of American Law*, pp. 340–41.

17. As cited ibid., p. 341.

18. As quoted in Swisher, *The Taney Period*, p. 349, n. 30.

19. As quoted by Mitchell, "The Federal Rules of Civil Procedure," p. 74.

20. See Sidney Post Simpson, "Fifty Years of American Equity," *Harvard Law Review* 50 (1936): 171.

21. Timothy Walker, "Law Reform in Missouri," *Western Law Journal* 6 (1849): 431. See also Swisher, *The Taney Period*, p. 349.

22. "Report of Commissioners Appointed to Revise and Reform the Procedure in the Courts of Justice of this Commonwealth," in *A Memoir of Benjamin Robbins Curtis*, ed., Benjamin R. Curtis, 2 vols. (Boston: Little, Brown, 1879), 2:149.

23. See Robert Millar, *Civil Procedure of the Trial Court in Historical Perspective* (New York: Law Center of New York University for the National Conference of Judicial Councils, 1952).

24. Friedman, *History of American Law*, p. 343.

25. Henry H. Ingersoll, "Some Anomalies of Practice," *Yale Law Journal* 1 (1891): 89, 91, 92, as quoted in Friedman, *History of American Law*, p. 344.

26. C. M. Hepburn, *The Historical Development of Code Pleading in America and England* (Cincinnati: W. H. Anderson, 1897), p. 18.

27. 17 Stat. 196.

28. Swisher, *The Taney Period*, p. 234.

29. *Malcolm* v. *Bayard*, 1 Johns. (N.Y.) 453, 471 (1806); and 19 Howard 162, 175 (1857).

30. Swisher, *The Taney Period*, p. 355.

31. Mitchell, "The Federal Rules of Civil Procedure," p. 75.

32. 28 U.S.C. s. 723b.

33. 28 U.S.C. s. 723c.

34. Mitchell, "The Federal Rules of Civil Procedure," p. 79.

35. Ibid.

36. 308 U.S. 645.

37. 7 Wheaton xvii.

38. 1 Howard xli.

39. 226 U.S. 627.

40. 308 U.S. 645, 649.

41. See chap. 2, above.

Chapter Six

1. *Briggs* v. *Elliott; Davis* v. *County School Board of Prince Edward County, Virginia; Gebhard* v. *Belton.*

2. See *Willard* v. *Tayloe;* see also Blackstone, *Commentaries on the Laws of England*, Kames, *Principles of Equity*, and Story, *Commentaries on Equity Jurisprudence*, passim.

3. But see also Graglia, *Disaster by Decree;* Robert Harris, *The Quest for Equality* (Baton Rouge: Louisiana State University Press, 1960); Alexander M. Bickel, "The Original Understanding of the Segregation Decision," *Harvard Law Review* 69 (1955): 1; and Berger, *Government by Judiciary.*

4. 347 U.S. 483, 489 n. 1, and 98 F. Supp. 797.

5. *Cruickshank* v. *Bidwell* and *Massachusetts State Grange* v. *Benton.*

6. The classic expression of the "evidence" Warren considered in determining the psychological damage to Negro children is found in Kenneth B. Clark, "The Effects of Segregation and the Consequences of Desegregation: A Social Science Statement," *Minnesota Law Review* 37 (1953): 427. Not only is such social-science evidence an inherently risky business for judicial decision-making, given the generally hypothetical nature of such research, but Clark's research was a particularly bad choice, given that it contained a fundamental flaw—a flaw clearly revealed in the data he presented. See Graglia, *Disaster by Decree,* pp. 27–29. See also Edmond Cahn, "Jurisprudence," *New York University Law Review* 30 (1955): 150; Monroe Berger, "Desegregation, Law, and Social Science," *Commentary* 23 (1957): 471; Herbert Garfinkel, "Social Science Evidence and the School Segregation Cases," *Journal of Politics* 21 (1959): 37; Ernest Van den Haag, "Social Science Testimony in the Desegregation Cases—A Reply to Professor Kenneth Clark," *Villanova Law Review* 6 (1960): 69; A. James Gregory, "The Law, Social Science and School Segregation: An Assessment," *Western Reserve Law Review* 14 (1963): 621; and Horowitz, *The Courts and Social Policy.*

7. *Federalist,* No. 10, p. 59. In elevating the social group to the level of constitutional principle, the Court, in effect, denied its own logic of only six years before; for in *Shelley* v. *Kraemer* the Court had held that "the rights created by the first section of the Fourteenth Amendment are by its terms guaranteed to the individual. The rights established are personal rights" (at 22). See Louis Lusky, "The Stereotype: Hardcore of Racism," *Buffalo Law Review* 13 (1963): 459.

8. *Willard* v. *Tayloe; Pennsylvania* v. *Williams.*

9. *Foster* v. *Mansfield, C. & L. M. R. Co.*

10. *Rees* v. *Watertown.*

11. Stone's opinion here was not the product of haste; he had been grappling with the vexatious issue of the public interest in equity cases since 1933; for in that year, in *United States ex rel. Greathouse* v. *Dern,* he noted that "a court of equity may refuse to enforce or protect legal rights, the exercise of which may be prejudicial to the public interst" (at 360). And, again in 1933, Stone held, in *Central Kentucky Natural Gas Co.* v. *Railroad Commission of Kentucky* (at 271), that there were "some limitations upon the extent to which a federal court of equity may properly go in prescribing ... relief, [limitations] which are inherent in the nature of the jurisdiction it exercises." Whereas federal courts could legitimately set aside a "confiscatory rate" as violative of the Fourteenth Amendment, they could not prescribe appropriate rates; such an action, because it was not within the judicial power conferred upon the federal courts by the Constitution, was reserved to the states. In 1937, Stone returned to the problem of delineating the public interest in equity proceedings and argued that "courts of equity may, and frequently do, go much farther both to give and to withhold relief in furtherance of

the public interest than they are accustomed to go when only private interests are involved" (*Virginia Railway Co.* v. *System Federation No. 40*, at 552). By 1939, Stone had formulated the traditional maxim concisely: "It is a familiar doctrine that the extent to which a court of equity may grant or withhold its aid, and the manner of moulding its remedies, may be affected by they public interest involved" (*United States* v. *Morgan*, at 194).

The general thrust of the notion of "public interest" in equity cases was that of judicial restraint. The cases that touched on the "public interest" doctrine assumed that the public laws represented the public interest and that the courts should be willing to defer to those established laws. Even when a "substantial constitutional issue" was tendered, it was held that the courts ought not to enter a "sensitive area of social policy" unless no alternative to its adjudication was open. The history of equity jurisdiction was seen as "the history of regard for the public consequences in employing the extraordinary remedy of the injunction" (*Railroad Commission of Texas* v. *Pullman Co.*, at 498, 500; *Harrisonville* v. *W. S. Dickey Clay Co.*, at 338). For the Court's view in the years preceding Mr. Justice Stone's opinions, see *Joy* v. *St. Louis*, in which it was stated that "the interests of the public are held to be controlling upon a court of equity," and *Beasley* v. *Texas & Pacific Railway*, in which Mr. Justice Holmes pointed to the hold the public interest was to have over courts of equity by noting that "if it appears that an injunction would be against public policy, the court properly may refuse to be made an instrument for such a result, whatever the pleadings" (at 498).

12. See also *David* v. *Gray* (at 220).

13. See also *Ex Parte Young* (at 167).

14. *In re Sawyer* (at 210).

15. See also *Miles* v. *Caldwell*.

16. See also *Pennsylvania* v. *Wheeling* (at 462); *Irvine* v. *Marshall*; and *Payne* v. *Hook*.

17. *United States* v. *Howland* (at 114).

18. *Livingston* v. *Story* (at 655).

19. See "Letters from the Federal Farmer" in *Storing*. See also chap. 2, above.

20. *Willard* v. *Tayloe* (at 567). See also *Bennett* v. *Butterworth* and *McFaul* v. *Ramsey*.

21. Story, "Chancery Jurisdiction," *Misc. Writings*, p. 167.

22. *Foster* v. *Mansfield, C. & L. M. R. Co.*

23. Kent, *Commentaries on American Law*, 1:321.

24. *Enelow* v. *New York Life Insurance Co.* (at 382).

25. *Sprague* v. *Ticonic National Bank* (at 169).

26. *Stainback* v. *Mo Hock Ke Lok Po* (at 382, n. 26).

27. *Graves* v. *Boston Marine Insurance Co.; Wright* v. *Ellison; Payne* v. *Hook.*

28. *Dows* v. *City of Chicago* (at 110–12); *Parker* v. *Winnipiseogee* (at 55); *Cruickshank* v. *Bidwell* (at 81); *Boise Artesian Hot and Cold Water* v. *Boise City* (at 281); *Massachusetts State Grange* v. *Benton; Walla Walla* v. *Walla Walla Water Co.* (at 11).

29. *Boise Artesian Hot and Cold Water* v. *Boise City* (at 282); *Walla Walla* v. *Walla Walla Water Co.* (at 11).

30. *Parker* v. *Winnipiseogee* (at 551).
31. *Cruickshank* v. *Bidwell* (at 81).
32. *Atlas Life Insurance* v. *W. I. Southern, Inc.* (at 570). See also *Enelow* v. *New York Life Insurance Co.; DiGiovanni* v. *Camden Fire Insurance Association;* and *American Life Insurance* v. *Stewart.*
33. *Massachusetts State Grange* v. *Benton* (at 527); *Fenner* v. *Boykin* (at 243).
34. *Gilchrist* v. *Interborough Rapid Transit* (at 207).
35. *Matthews* v. *Rodgers* (at 525).
36. *Hawks* v. *Hamill* (at 60, 61).
37. *Pennsylvania* v. *Williams* (at 182).
38. *Petroleum Exploration Inc.* v. *Public Service Commission of Kentucky* (at 218); *Beal* v. *Missouri Pacific Railroad Corporation* (at 50); *Railroad Commission of Texas* v. *Pullman Co.* (at 500).
39. See Berger, *Government by Judiciary,* passim.
40. *Texas and Pacific Railway Co.* v. *Chicago, R. I. & P. R. Co.* (at 406); *Virginia Railway Co.* v. *System Federation No. 40* (at 551). See, especially, *Central Kentucky Natural Gas Co.* v. *Railroad Commission of Kentucky* (at 271).
41. Cardozo, *The Nature of the Judicial Process,* p. 51.
42. *Railroad Commission of Texas* v. *Pullman Co.*

Chapter Seven

1. See Philip B. Kurland, *Politics, the Constitution, and the Warren Court* (Chicago: University of Chicago Press, 1971).
2. *New Orleans City Park Improvement Association* v. *Detiege.*
3. *State Athletic Commission* v. *Dorsey.*
4. *Turner* v. *Memphis.*
5. *Johnson* v. *Virginia.*
6. *Schiro* v. *Bynum.* For a comprehensive account of the Court's expansion of the *Brown* principle, see Abraham, *Freedom and the Court,* pp. 343–440.
7. See 100 *Congressional Record* 1518 ff.
8. See Graglia, *Disaster by Decree,* pp. 46–66, for examples of assurances by the bill's floor leaders during the legislative debates that mandatory integration was not within the scope of the legislation.
9. 42 U.S.C. 2000 (c).
10. The guidelines are reprinted in an appendix to *Price* v. *Dennison Independent School District Board of Education,* 348 F. 2d 1010, 1015 (1965).
11. See Graglia, *Disaster by Decree,* pp. 46–66.
12. *Bradley* v. *School Board City of Richmond* (at 105).
13. *Certiorari* denied, 389 U.S. 840 (1967).
14. See Graglia, *Disaster by Decree,* p. 59.
15. 380 F. 2d 385 (1967).
16. Graglia, *Disaster by Decree,* p. 90. See also Glazer, *Affirmative Discrimination;* Kurland, *Politics, the Constitution, and the Warren Court;* Abraham, *Freedom and the Court;* and Alexander M. Bickel, *Politics and the Warren Court* (New York: Harper & Row, 1968).

17. *Singleton* v. *Jackson Municipal Separate School District,* 419 F. 2d 1211, 1216, 1217 (1970).
18. Graglia, *Disaster by Decree,* p. 66.
19. *United States* v. *Scotland Neck City Board of Education* and *Wright* v. *Council City of Emporia.*
20. *Bradley* v. *State Board of Education of the Commonwealth of Virginia.* See also Abraham, *Freedom and the Court,* pp. 378–86.

Epilogue

1. *Federalist,* No. 78, p. 524.
2. Ibid.
3. Ibid.
4. Ibid., pp. 525–26.
5. Ibid., p. 526.
6. *Federalist,* No. 51, p. 351.
7. *Federalist,* No. 81, p. 546.
8. *Federalist,* No. 78, p. 523.
9. James Wilson, speech in the Philadelphia Convention, *Farrand,* 2:125.
10. James Madison, speeches in the Philadelphia Convention, *Farrand,* 1:422, 462. For other remarks of a similar nature, by Madison and Gouverneur Morris, see *Farrand,* 2:126, 361.
11. *Federalist,* Nos. 14, 37, 53, 63, 78.
12. *Federalist,* No. 49, p. 340.
13. *Federalist,* No. 43, p. 296.
14. *Federalist,* No. 14, p. 89.
15. *Federalist,* No. 49, p. 340.
16. *Federalist,* No. 78.
17. Kurland, *Politics, the Constitution, and the Warren Court,* p. 86.
18. 19 Howard 393 (1857). See Don E. Fehrenbacher, *The Dred Scott Case: Its Significance in American Law and Politics* (New York: Oxford University Press, 1978), for the most recent and apparently definitive treatment of this landmark case.
19. As quoted in Abraham, *The Judicial Process,* p. 324.
20. Max Friedman, *Roosevelt and Frankfurter: Their Correspondence, 1928–1945* (Boston: Little, Brown, 1968), p. 383.
21. Dissenting opinion in *Harper* v. *Virginia Board of Elections* (at 678).
22. Kurland, *Politics, the Constitution, and the Warren Court,* p. xiv.
23. Sotirios A. Barber, *The Constitution and the Delegation of Congressional Power* (Chicago: University of Chicago Press, 1974), p. 8.
24. Ibid.
25. Ibid., p. 9.
26. *Federalist,* No. 37, p. 233.
27. See Bernard Bailyn, *The Ideological Origins of the American Revolution* (Cambridge, Mass.: Harvard University Press, 1967), and Martin Diamond, "The Declaration and the Constitution: Liberty, Democracy, and the Founders," in

Nathan Glazer and Irving Kristol, eds., *The American Commonwealth: 1976* (New York: Basic Books, 1976).

28. *Federalist,* Nos. 10 and 51. See also Martin Diamond, "Democracy and *The Federalist:* A Reconsideration of the Framers' Intents," *American Political Science Review* 53 (1959): 52.

29. *Federalist,* No. 10, p. 57.

30. Ibid., pp. 60–61.

31. *Federalist,* No. 9, p. 51.

32. *Federalist,* No. 78, p. 524.

33. Ibid., p. 528.

34. *Federalist,* No. 10, p. 57.

35. On the movement of the Court toward abandoning the "separate but equal" doctrine, see Harris, *Quest for Equality;* Abraham, *Freedom and the Court;* and Berger, *Government by Judiciary.* Consider also the opinions of the Court in *Missouri ex rel. Gaines* v. *Canada,* 305 U.S. 337 (1938); *Sipuel* v. *Oklahoma,* 332 U.S. 631 (1948); *Sweatt* v. *Painter,* 339 U.S. 629 (1950); and *McLaurin* v. *Oklahoma State Regents,* 339 U.S. 637 (1950). On the debates over the Fourteenth Amendment, see Alfred Avins, ed., *The Reconstruction Amendments Debates* (Richmond: Virginia Commission on Constitutional Government, 1967).

36. *Federalist,* No. 81.

37. The Constitution was viewed by its creators as a means of securing personal political liberty, not as a means of forcing an artificial equality of condition. Such men as Elbridge Gerry early in the Philadelphia Convention warned of the "danger of the levilling [*sic*] spirit" and the "evils" which often "flow from the excess of democracy." Such a leveling spirit was considered generally to be the antithesis of political liberty and private rights. And even though history and recent experience supported Charles Pinckney when he observed that among the peoples of the United States "there are fewer distinctions of fortunes & less of rank, than among the inhabitants of any other nation," it was clear to some that America was still not "one homogeneous mass, in which everything that affects a part will affect in the same manner the whole." As James Madison explained:

> In all civilized Countries the people fall into different classes havg. a real or supposed difference of interests. There will be creditors & debtors, farmers, merchts. & manufacturers. There will be particularly the distinction of rich & poor. It was true as had been observed [by Mr. Pinckney] we had not among us those hereditary distinctions which were a great source of the contests in the ancient Govts. as well as the modern States of Europe, nor those extremes of wealth and poverty which characterize the latter . . . . In framing a system which we intend to last for ages, we shd. not lose sight of the changes which ages will produce. An increase in population will of necessity increase the proportion of those who will labor under the hardships of life & secretly sigh for a more equal distribution of its blessings.

The solution for this hard political fact was not to attempt to reduce mankind to a homogeneous mass but rather to encourage such a diversity and multiplicity of interests that a majority faction would be rendered highly improbable. See *Ferrand,* 1:48, 398, 422, and *Federalist,* Nos. 10 and 51.

38. See, for example, *United States* v. *City of Parma*.

39. *Federalist*, No. 51, p. 349.

40. *Federalist*, No. 78.

41. *Federalist*, No. 81.

42. Story, "The Science of Government," *Misc. Writings*, p. 619.

43. As quoted in Joseph P. Lash, *From the Diaries of Felix Frankfurter* (New York: W. W. Norton, 1975), p. 54.

44. Berger, *Government by Judiciary*, p. 415.

45. Ibid., p. 413.

46. *Federalist*, Nos. 10, 51, 63, 70.

47. Berger, *Government by Judiciary*, p. 415.

48. Abraham Lincoln, *First Inaugural Address*, March 4, 1861.

List of Cases

Albemarle Paper Co. v. Moody, 422 U.S. 405 (1975).

Alexander v. Hillman, 296 U.S. 222 (1935).

Alexander v. Holmes County Board of Education, 396 U.S. 19 (1969).

American Life Insurance v. Stewart, 300 U.S. 203 (1937).

Atlas Life Insurance v. W. I. Southern, Inc., 306 U.S. 563 (1939).

Bangor Punta Operations, Inc. v. Bangor & Aroostook Railroad Co., 417 U.S. 703 (1974).

Barber v. Barber, 21 Howard 582 (1858).

Barbier v. Connolly, 113 U.S. 27 (1885).

Beacon Theatres, Inc. v. Westover, 359 U.S. 500 (1959).

Beal v. Missouri Pacific Railroad Corporation, 312 U.S. 45 (1941).

Beasley v. Texas & Pacific Railway Co., 191 U.S. 492 (1903).

Bell v. City School of Gary, Indiana, 324 F. 2d 209 (1963).

Bennett v. Butterworth, 11 Howard 669 (1850).

Boise Artesian Hot and Cold Water Co. v. Boise City, 213 U.S. 276 (1909).

Boyce's Executors v. Grundy, 3 Peters 210 (1830).

Boyle v. Zacharie and Turner, 6 Peters 648 (1832).

Bradley v. School Board of City of Richmond, 412 U.S. 92 (1973).

Brown v. Board of Education of Topeka, 347 U.S. 483 (1954).

Brown v. Board of Education of Topeka, 349 U.S. 294 (1955).

Brown v. Swann, 10 Peters 497 (1836).

Camp v. Boyd, 229 U.S. 530 (1913)

Carter v. West Feliciana Parish School Board, 396 U.S. 290 (1970).

List of Cases

Central Kentucky Natural Gas Co. v. Railroad Commission of Kentucky, 290 U.S. 264 (1933).

Crane v. Johnson, 242 U.S. 339 (1917).

Creath v. Sims, 5 Howard 191 (1847).

Cruickshank v. Bidwell, 176 U.S. 73 (1900).

Dairy Queen v. Wood, 369 U.S. 469 (1963).

Davis v. Gray, 16 Wallace 203 (1872).

DiGiovanni v. Camden Fire Insurance Association, 296 U.S. 63 (1935).

Dows v. City of Chicago, 11 Wallace 108 (1870).

DuPont v. Vance, 19 Howard 162 (1857).

Enelow v. New York Life Insurance Co., 293 U.S. 379 (1935).

Fenner v. Boykin, 271 U.S. 240 (1926).

Foster v. Mansfield, Coldwater & Lake Michigan Railroad Co., 146 U.S. 88 (1892).

Franks v. Bowman Transportation Co., 424 U.S. 747 (1976).

Gaines v. Relf, 15 Peters 9 (1841).

Gilchrist v. Interborough Rapid Transit, 279 U.S. 159 (1929).

Goss v. Board of Education of Knoxville, Tennessee, 373 U.S. 683 (1963).

Graves v. Boston Marine Insurance Co., 2 Cranch 418 (1805).

Green v. County School Board of New Kent County, 391 U.S. 430 (1968).

Griffin v. County School Board of Prince Edward County, 377 U.S. 218 (1964).

Hague v. Committee for Industrial Organization, 307 U.S. 496 (1939).

Harper v. Virginia Board of Elections, 383 U.S. 663 (1966).

Harrisonville v. W. S. Dickey Clay Co., 289 U.S. 334 (1933).

Hawks v. Hamill, 288 U.S. 52 (1933).

Hayburn's Case, 2 Dallas 409 (1792).

Hecht Co. v. Bowles, 321 U.S. 321 (1943).

Heine v. The Levee Commissioners, 19 Wallace 655 (1873).

Hills v. Gautreaux, 425 U.S. 284 (1976).

International News Service v. Associated Press, 248 U.S. 215 (1918).

Irvine v. Marshall, 20 Howard 558 (1858).

Johnson v. Towsley, 13 Wallace 72 (1871).

Johnson v. Virginia, 373 U.S. 61 (1963).

Joy v. St. Louis, 138 U.S. 47 (1891).

Keyes v. School District No. 1, Denver, Colorado, 413 U.S. 189 (1972).

Kugler v. Helfant, 421 U.S. 117 (1975).

Lau v. Nichols, 414 U.S. 563 (1974).

Lemon v. Kurtzman, 411 U.S. 192 (1973).

Livingston v. Story, 9 Peters 632 (1835).

Louisiana v. United States, 380 U.S. 145 (1965).

McChord v. Louisville, 183 U.S. 483 (1902).

McFaul v. Ramsey, 20 Howard 523 (1858).

Massachusetts State Grange v. Benton, 272 U.S. 525 (1926).

Matthews v. Rodgers, 284 U.S. 521 (1932).

Meredith v. Winter Haven, 320 U.S. 228 (1943).

Miles v. Caldwell, 2 Wallace 35 (1864).

Milliken v. Bradley, 418 U.S. 717 (1974).

Milliken v. Bradley, 433 U.S. 267 (1977).

Mitchell v. Robert De Mario Jewelry, Inc., 361 U.S. 288 (1960).

Morgantown v. Royal Insurance Co., 337 U.S. 254 (1949).

New Orleans City Park Improvement Association v. Detiege, 358 U.S. 54 (1958).

Northcross v. Board of Education of Memphis, Tennessee, City Schools, 397 U.S. 232 (1970).

Osborn v. Bank of the United States, 9 Wheaton 738 (1824).

Packard v. Banton, 264 U.S. 140 (1924).

Parker v. Winnipiseogee, 2 Black 545 (1862).

Parsons v. Bedford, 3 Peters 433 (1830).

Pasadena City Board of Education v. Spangler, 427 U.S. 424 (1976).

Payne v. Hook, 7 Wallace 425 (1868).

Pennsylvania v. Wheeling, 18 Howard 460 (1855).

Pennsylvania v. Williams, 294 U.S. 176 (1935).

Petroleum Exploration Inc. v. Public Service Commission of Kentucky, 304 U.S. 209 (1938).

Philadelphia Co. v. Stimson, 223 U.S. 605 (1912).

Plessy v. Ferguson, 163 U.S. 537 (1896).

Porter v. Warner, 328 U.S. 395 (1946).

Railroad Commission of Texas v. Pullman Co., 312 U.S. 496 (1941).

List of Cases

Rees v. Watertown, 19 Wallace 107 (1873).

Rizzo v. Goode, 423 U.S. 362 (1976).

Robinson v. Campbell, 3 Wheaton 212 (1818).

Ross v. Bernhard, 396 U.S. 531 (1970).

Russell v. Todd, 309 U.S. 280 (1940).

In re Sawyer, 124 U.S. 200 (1888).

Schiro v. Bynum, 375 U.S. 395 (1964).

Shelley v. Kraemer, 334 U.S. 1 (1948).

Shelton v. Platt, 139 U.S. 591 (1891).

Singleton v. Jackson Municipal Separate School District, 419 F. 2d 1211 (1965).

Sixty-Seventh Minnesota State Senate v. Beens, 406 U.S. 187 (1972).

Sprague v. Ticonic National Bank, 307 U.S. 161 (1939).

Stainback v. Mo Hock Ke Lok Po, 336 U.S. 368 (1949).

State Athletic Commission v. Dorsey, 359 U.S. 533 (1959).

Stratton v. St. Louis Southwestern Railway Co., 284 U.S. 530 (1932).

Swann v. Charlotte-Mecklenburg Board of Education, 402 U.S. 1 (1971).

Terrace v. Thompson, 263 U.S. 197 (1923).

Texas and Pacific Railway Co. v. Marshall, 136 U.S. 393 (1890).

Truax v. Raich, 239 U.S. 33 (1915).

Turner v. Memphis, 369 U.S. 350 (1962).

Union Pacific Railway Co. v. Chicago, Rock Island and Pacific Railway Co., 163 U.S. 564 (1896).

United States v. American Friends Service Committee, 419 U.S. 7 (1974).

United States *ex rel.* Greathouse v. Dern, 289 U.S. 352 (1933).

United States v. Howland, 4 Wheaton 108 (1819).

United States v. Jefferson County Board of Education, 372 F. 2d 836 (1966).

United States v. Montgomery County Board of Education, 395 U.S. 225 (1969).

United States v. Morgan, 307 U.S. 183 (1939).

United States v. City of Parma, 504 F. Supp. 913 (1980).

United States v. Scotland Neck City Board of Education, 407 U.S. 484 (1972).

Virginia Railway Co. v. System Federation No. 40, 300 U.S. 515 (1937).

Walla Walla v. Walla Walla Water Co., 172 U.S. 1 (1898).

List of Cases

Willard v. Tayloe, 8 Wallace 557 (1869).
Wright v. Council of City of Emporia, 407 U.S. 451 (1972).
Wright v. Ellison, 1 Wallace 16 (1863).
Wylie v. Coxe, 15 Howard 415 (1853).
Ex parte Young, 209 U.S. 123 (1908).

Bibliography

Primary Sources
Books

Aristotle. *Magna Moralia*. Translated by G. Cyril Armstrong. Loeb Classical Library. Cambridge, Mass.: Harvard University Press, 1935.
———. *Nicomachean Ethics*. Translated by H. Rackham. Loeb Classical Library. Cambridge, Mass.: Harvard University Press, 1934.
———. *Politics*. Translated by H. Rackham. Loeb Classical Library. Cambridge, Mass.: Harvard University Press, 1932.
———. *Rhetoric*. Translated by J. H. Freese. Loeb Classical Library. Cambridge, Mass.: Harvard University Press, 1926.
Bacon, Francis. *The Works of Francis Bacon*. Edited by James Spedding. 7 vols. London: Longman, 1879.
———. *Law Tracts*. 22d ed. Savoy: Dan Brown, 1741.
Ballow, Henry. *A Treatise of Equity*. Edited by John Fonblanque. 2 vols. Philadelphia: A. Small, 1820.
Blackstone, William. *Commentaries on the Laws of England*. 2 vols. 15th ed. London: A. Strahan, 1809.
Bracton, Henrici de. *De Legibus et Consuetudinibus Angliae*. Edited by Travers Twiss. 4 vols. London: Longman, 1878.
Cardozo, Benjamin N. *The Nature of the Judicial Process*. New Haven: Yale University Press, 1921.
Cicero. *Ad Herennium*. Translated by H. Caplan. Loeb Classical Library. Cambridge, Mass.: Harvard University Press, 1952.

————. *De Legibus*. Translated by C. W. Keyes. Loeb Classical Library. Cambridge, Mass.: Harvard University Press, 1928.

————. *De Officiis*. Translated by Walter Miller. Loeb Classical Library. Cambridge, Mass.: Harvard University Press, 1913.

Coke, Sir Edward. *The First Part of the Institutes of the Laws of England*. Edited by Charles Butler. 2 vols. Philadelphia: Robert M. Small, 1853.

DuPonceau, Peter S. *A Dissertation on the Nature and Extent of the Jurisdiction of the Courts of the United States*. Philadelphia: A. Small, 1824.

Fortesque, Sir John. *De Laudibus Legum Angliae*. Edited by S. G. Chrimes. Cambridge, Eng.: At the University Press, 1942.

Glanville, Ranulph de. *De Legibus et Consuetudinibus Regni Angliae*. Edited by G. D. G. Hall. London: Thomas Nelson & Sons, 1965.

Goodenow, John Milton. *Historical Sketches of the Principles and Maxims of American Jurisprudence in Contrast with the Doctrines of the English Common Law on the Subject of Crimes and Punishments*. Steubenville, Ohio: James Wilson, 1819.

Gould, James. *A Treatise on the Principles of Pleading in Civil Actions*. Boston: Lilly & Wait, 1832.

Hamilton, Alexander; James Madison; and John Jay. *The Federalist*. Edited by Jacob Cooke. Middletown, Conn.: Wesleyan University Press, 1962.

Hilliard, Francis. *The Elements of Law*. Boston: Hilliard, Gray, 1835.

Hobbes, Thomas. *A Dialogue between a Philosopher and a Student of the Common Laws of England*. Edited by Joseph Cropsey. Chicago: University of Chicago Press, 1971.

————. *The Elements of Law*. Edited by Ferdinand Tönnies. 2d ed. New York: Barnes & Noble, 1969.

————. *Leviathan*. Oxford: Oxford University Press, 1909.

Home, Henry, Lord Kames. *Principles of Equity*. 7th ed. Edinburgh: Bell & Bradfute, 1825.

Justinian. *Institutes*. Edited by Thomas Cooper; translated by G. Harris. Philadelphia: P. Byrne, 1812.

Kent, James. *Commentaries on American Law*. 4 vols. New York: O. Halsted, 1826.

Maine, Henry Sumner. *Ancient Law*. 2d ed. London: John Murray, 1863.

Maitland, Frederic W. *Equity*. Cambridge, Eng.: At the University Press, 1936.

St. Germain, Christopher. *Dialogues between a Doctor of Divinity and a Student of the Laws of England*. Edited by W. Muchall. Cincinnati: Robert Clarke, 1874.

Smith, Adam. *Lectures on Jurisprudence*. Edited by R. L. Meek, D. D. Raphael, and P. G. Stein. Oxford: Oxford University Press, 1978.

Story, Joseph. *Commentaries on the Constitution of the United States*. 3 vols. Boston: Hilliard, Gray, 1833.

————. *Commentaries on Equity Jurisprudence.* 2 vols. 3d ed. Boston: Little & Brown, 1842.

————. *Commentaries on Equity Pleadings.* 3d ed. Boston: Little & Brown, 1844.

Taylor, John. *Elements of Civil Law.* 4th ed. London: S. Sweet, 1828.

Tocqueville, Alexis de. *Democracy in America.* Edited by J. P. Mayer; translated by George Lawrence. New York: Harper & Row, 1966.

Collected Works and Correspondence

Ames, Fisher. *Works of Fisher Ames.* Edited by Seth Ames. 2 vols. Boston: Little, Brown, 1854.

Field, David Dudley. *Speeches, Arguments and Miscellaneous Papers of David Dudley Field.* Edited by A. P. Strague. 3 vols. New York: D. Appleton, 1884–90.

Hamilton, Alexander. *The Law Practice of Alexander Hamilton.* Edited by Julius Goebel, Jr. 2 vols. New York: Columbia University Press, 1964.

Jefferson, Thomas. *The Writings of Thomas Jefferson.* Edited by Paul L. Ford. 10 vols. New York: G. P. Putnam's Sons, 1892–99.

————. *The Writings of Thomas Jefferson.* Library Edition. 20 vols. New York, 1903.

————. *The Papers of Thomas Jefferson.* Edited by Julian P. Boyd. Princeton: Princeton University Press, 1950————.

Madison, James. *The Writings of James Madison.* Edited by Gaillard Hunt. 9 vols. New York: G. P. Putnam's Sons, 1900–1910.

————. *The Papers of James Madison.* 13 vols. Vols. 1–7, edited by William T. Hutchinson and William M. E. Rachal; vols. 8–9, edited by Robert A. Rutland and William M. E. Rachal; vols. 10–11, edited by Robert A. Rutland and Charles F. Hobson. Volumes 1–10, Chicago: University of Chicago Press, 1962–77. Volumes 11–13, Charlottesville: University of Virginia Press, 1978–81.

Story, Joseph. *The Miscellaneous Writings of Joseph Story.* Edited by W. W. Story. Boston: Little & Brown, 1852.

————. *The Life and Letters of Joseph Story.* Edited by W. W. Story. 2 vols. Boston: Little & Brown, 1851.

Wilson, James. *The Works of James Wilson.* Edited by Robert G. McCloskey. 2 vols. Cambridge, Mass.: Harvard University Press, 1967.

Documents and Records

Annals of the Congress of the United States, 1789–1875. 10 vols. Washington, D.C., 1834–56.

Antifederalists, The. Edited by Cecelia M. Kenyon. Indianapolis: Bobbs-Merrill, 1966.

Complete Anti-Federalist, The. Edited by Herbert J. Storing. 7 vols. Chicago: University of Chicago Press, 1981.

Debates in the Several State Conventions on the Adoption of the Federal Constitution, The. Edited by Jonathan Elliot. 5 vols. Philadelphia: J. B. Lippincott, 1896.

Journal of William Maclay, The. Edited by E. S. Maclay. New York: Albert & Charles Boni, 1927.

Pennsylvania and the Federal Constitution, 1787–1788. Edited by John Bach McMaster and Frederick D. Stone. 2 vols. Philadelphia: Historical Society of Pennsylvania, 1888.

Principles and Acts of the Revolution in America. Edited by Hezekiah Niles. New York, 1876.

Public Statutes at Large of the United States of America, 1789–1845, The. Edited by Richard Peters. Published by authority of Congress. 5 vols. Boston: Little, Brown, 1850.

Reconstruction Amendments' Debates, The. Edited by Alfred Avins. Richmond: Virginia Commission on Constitutional Government, 1967.

Records of the Federal Convention of 1787, The. Edited by Max Farrand. 4 vols. New Haven: Yale University Press, 1937.

Reports of Cases Signed and Adjudged in the Superior Court of Judicature of Massachusetts Bay, 1761–1772. Edited by Josiah Quincy. Boston, 1865.

Secondary Sources
Books

Abraham, Henry J. *Freedom and the Court.* 3d ed. New York: Oxford University Press, 1977.

———. *The Judicial Process.* 4th ed. New York: Oxford University Press, 1980.

———. *The Judiciary.* 5th ed. Boston: Allyn & Bacon, 1980.

———. *Justices and Presidents.* New York: Oxford University Press, 1974.

Ames, James Barr. *Lectures on Legal History.* Cambridge, Mass.: Harvard University Press, 1913.

Association of American Law Schools. *Select Essays in Anglo-American Legal History.* 3 vols. Boston: Little, Brown, 1907.

Bailyn, Bernard. *The Ideological Origins of the American Revolution.* Cambridge, Mass.: Harvard University Press, 1967.

Barber, Sotirios A. *The Constitution and the Delegation of Congressional Power.* Chicago: University of Chicago Press, 1975.

Berger, Raoul. *Government by Judiciary.* Cambridge, Mass.: Harvard University Press, 1977.

Berns, Walter. *The First Amendment and the Future of American Democracy.* New York: Basic Books, 1976.

Bickel, Alexander M. *The Least Dangerous Branch.* Indianapolis: Bobbs-Merrill, 1963.

———. *The Morality of Consent.* New Haven: Yale University Press, 1976.

———. *The Supreme Court and the Idea of Progress.* New York: Harper & Row, 1970.

Bodenheimer, Edgar. *Jurisprudence: The Philosophy and Methods of the Law.* Cambridge, Mass.: Harvard University Press, 1974.

Choper, Jesse. *Judicial Review and the National Political Process.* Chicago: University of Chicago Press, 1980.

Corwin, Edward S. *The "Higher" Law Background of American Constitutional Law.* Ithaca, N.Y.: Cornell University Press, 1955.

Crosskey, William W. *Politics and the Constitution.* 3 vols. Chicago: University of Chicago Press, 1980.

Dunne, Gerald T. *Joseph Story and the Rise of the Supreme Court.* New York: Simon & Schuster, 1970.

Eidelberg, Paul. *The Philosophy of the American Constitution.* New York: The Free Press, 1968.

Elliott, Ward E. Y. *The Rise of Guardian Democracy.* Cambridge, Mass.: Harvard University Press, 1974.

Ellis, Richard E. *The Jeffersonian Crisis: Courts and Politics in the Young Republic.* New York: Oxford University Press, 1971.

Ely, John Hart. *Democracy and Distrust.* Cambridge, Mass.: Harvard University Press, 1980.

Essays in Anglo-Saxon Law. Boston: Little, Brown, 1876.

Faulkner, Robert K. *The Jurisprudence of John Marshall.* Princeton: Princeton University Press, 1968.

Fiss, Owen M. *The Civil Rights Injunction.* Bloomington: Indiana University Press, 1978.

Friedman, Lawrence M. *A History of American Law.* New York: Simon & Schuster, 1973.

Goebel, Julius Jr. *History of the Supreme Court of the United States: Antecedents and Beginnings to 1801.* Volume 1 of the Oliver Wendell Holmes Devise. New York: Macmillan, 1971.

Goldwin, Robert A., ed. *How Democratic Is America?* Chicago: Rand McNally, 1964.

Glazer, Nathan. *Affirmative Discrimination.* New York: Basic Books, 1974.

Graglia, Lino A. *Disaster by Decree.* Ithaca, N.Y.: Cornell University Press, 1976.

Hamburger, Max. *Morals and Law: The Growth of Aristotle's Legal Theory.* New York: Biblo & Tannen, 1965.

Harris, Robert J. *The Judicial Power of the United States.* Baton Rouge: Louisiana State University Press, 1940.

———. *The Quest for Equality.* Baton Rouge: Louisiana State University Press, 1960.

Heron, D. Caulfield. *An Introduction to the History of Jurisprudence.* London: John Parker & Son, 1860.

Horowitz, Donald L. *The Courts and Social Policy.* Washington, D.C.: The Brookings Institution, 1977.

Horwitz, Morton J. *The Transformation of American Law: 1780–1860*. Cambridge, Mass.: Harvard University Press, 1977.

Horwitz, Robert H., ed. *The Moral Foundations of the American Republic*. Charlottesville: University Press of Virginia, 1977.

Jaffa, Harry V. *The Conditions of Freedom*. Baltimore: Johns Hopkins University Press, 1975.

Kluger, Richard. *Simple Justice*. New York: Random House, 1975.

Kristol, Irving, and Nathan Glazer, eds. *The American Commonwealth: 1976*. New York: Basic Books, 1976.

Kristol, William. "The American Judicial Power and the American Regime." Ph.D. dissertation, Harvard University, 1979.

Kurland, Philip B. *Politics, the Constitution, and the Warren Court*. Chicago: University of Chicago Press, 1970.

————, ed. *The Supreme Court Review*. Chicago: University of Chicago Press, 1960————.

Lowi, Theodore J. *The End of Liberalism*. New York: W. W. Norton, 1969.

Lusky, Louis. *By What Right?* Charlottesville, Va.: Michie, 1975.

McClellan, James P. *Joseph Story and the American Constitution*. Norman: University of Oklahoma Press, 1971.

Mark, Irving. *Agrarian Conflicts in Colonial New York: 1711–1775*. New York: Friedman, 1940.

Meyers, Marvin. *The Jacksonian Persausion*. Stanford, Calif.: Stanford University Press, 1957.

Parkes, Joseph. *A History of the Court of Chancery*. London: Longman, 1828.

Plucknett, Theodore F. T. *A Concise History of the Common Law*. 5th ed. Boston: Little, Brown, 1956.

Pollock, Sir Frederick. *Essays in the Law*. London: Macmillan, 1922.

Re, Edward D., ed. *Selected Essays on Equity*. New York: Oceana Publications, 1955.

————. *Equity and Equitable Remedies: Cases and Materials*. 5th ed. Mineola, N.Y.: Foundation Press, 1975.

Reppy, Alison, ed. *David Dudley Field: Centenary Essays*. New York: New York University School of Law, 1949.

Rossum, Ralph A. "The Federal Pyramid: The Political Thought of James Wilson." Ph.D. dissertation, University of Chicago, 1973.

————. *Reverse Discrimination*. New York: Marcel-Dekker, 1980.

Rutland, Robert A. *The Birth of the Bill of Rights, 1776–1791*. Chapel Hill: University of North Carolina Press, 1955.

————. *The Ordeal of the Constitution*. Norman: University of Oklahoma Press, 1966.

Schultze, Charles L. *The Public Use of Private Interest*. Washington, D.C.: The Brookings Institution, 1977.

Smith, James Morton. *Freedom's Fetters: The Alien and Sedition Laws and Civil Liberties*. Ithaca, N.Y.: Cornell University Press, 1956.

Strauss, Leo. *Natural Right and History*. Chicago: University of Chicago Press, 1953.

————. *The Political Philosophy of Hobbes*. Chicago: University of Chicago Press, 1936.

————, and Joseph Cropsey, eds. *History of Political Philosophy*. 2d ed. Chicago: Rand McNally, 1972.

Swisher, Carl B. *American Constitutional Development*. Boston: Houghton Mifflin, 1943.

————. *The Growth of Constitutional Power in the United States*. Chicago: University of Chicago Press, 1946.

————. *History of the Supreme Court of the United States: The Taney Period, 1936–1964*. Volume 5 of the Oliver Wendell Holmes Devise. New York: Macmillan, 1974.

Thayer, James Bradley. *Legal Essays*. Cambridge, Mass.: Harvard University Press, 1927.

Tribe, Laurence. *American Constitutional Law*. Mineola, N.Y.: Foundation Press, 1977.

Warren, Charles. *A History of the American Bar*. Boston: Little, Brown, 1911.

————. *The Supreme Court in United States History*. 2 vols. Boston: Little, Brown, 1922.

Wilkinson, J. Harvie, III. *From "Brown" to "Bakke."* New York: Oxford University Press, 1979.

Wood, Gordon S. *The Creation of the American Republic: 1776–1787*. Chapel Hill: University of North Carolina Press, 1969.

Zetterbaum, Marvin. *Tocqueville and the Problem of Democracy*. Stanford, Calif.: Stanford University Press, 1967.

Articles and Pamphlets

Adams, George Burton. "The Origin of English Equity." *Columbia Law Review* 16 (1916): 84.

Bickel, Alexander M. "The Original Understanding of the Segregation Decision." *Harvard Law Review* 69 (1955): 1.

Bordwell, Percy. "The Resurgence of Equity." *University of Chicago Law Review* 1 (1934): 741.

Brice, Charles S. "Roman Aequitas and English Equity." *Georgetown Law Journal* 2 (1913): 16.

Cahn, Edmond. "Jurisprudence." *New York University Law Review* 30 (1955): 150.

Chayes, Abram. "The Role of the Judge in Public Law Litigation." *Harvard Law Review* 89 (1976): 1281.

Cook, Walter Wheeler. "The Powers of Courts of Equity." *Columbia Law Review* 15 (1925): 1.

Clark, Charles E. "The Union of Law and Equity." *Columbia Law Review* 25 (1925): 1.

Clark, Kenneth B. "The Effects of Segregation and the Consequences of

Desegregation: A Social Science Statement." *Minnesota Law Review* 37 (1953): 427.

Coe, M. V., and L. W. Morse. "Chonology of the Development of the David Dudley Field Code." *Cornell Law Quarterly* 27 (1942): 238.

Diamond, Martin. "Democracy and *The Federalist:* A Reconsideration of the Framers' Intents." *American Political Science Review* 53 (1959): 52.

————. *The Revolution of Sober Expectations.* Washington, D.C.: American Enterprise Institute, 1974.

Emmerglick, Leonard J. "A Century of the New Equity." *Texas Law Review* 23 (1945): 244.

Garfinkel, Herbert. "Social Science Evidence and the School Segregation Cases." *Journal of Politics* 21 (1959): 37.

Gregor, A. James. "The Law, Social Science and School Segregation: An Assessment." *Western Reserve Law Review* 14 (1963): 621.

Hohfield, Wesley N. "The Relations between Equity and Law." *Michigan Law Review* 11 (1913): 553.

Hook, Sidney. "The Road to a University 'Quota' System." *Freedom at Issue* 12 (1972): 21.

Kennedy, Duncan. "Form and Substance in Private Law Adjudication." *Harvard Law Review* 89 (1976): 1685.

Kurland, Philip B. "The Supreme Court, 1963 Term Foreword: Equal in Origin and Equal in Title to the Legislative and Executive Branches of the Government." *Harvard Law Review* 78 (1964): 143.

————. "'Brown v. Board of Education was the Beginning': The School Desegregation Cases in the United States Supreme Court; 1954–1979." *Washington University Law Quarterly* (1979): 309.

Pound, Roscoe. "Common Law and Legislation." *Harvard Law Review* 21 (1908): 383.

————. "Equitable Relief against Defamation and Injuries to Personality." Ibid. 29 (1916): 640.

————. "Progress of the Law, 1918–1919: Equity." Ibid. 33 (1920): 420, 813, 929.

————. "The Maxims of Equity." Ibid. 34 (1921): 809.

Rossum, Ralph A. "Representation and Republican Government: Contemporary Court Variations on the Founders' Theme." *American Journal of Jurisprudence* 28 (1978): 88.

————. "Ameliorative Racial Preference and the Fourteenth Amendment: Some Constitutional Problems." *Journal of Politics* 38 (1976): 346.

————. "The Supreme Court and the Teaching of Political Responsibility." In Gary L. McDowell, ed., *Taking the Constitution Seriously.* Dubuque: Kendall-Hunt Publishing Co., 1981.

Simpson, Sidney Post. "Fifty Years of American Equity." *Harvard Law Review* 50 (1936): 171.

Storing, Herbert J. "William Blackstone." In Leo Strauss and Joseph Cropsey, eds., *History of Political Philosophy*. 2d ed. Chicago: Rand McNally, 1972.

Story, Joseph. *A Discourse on the Past History, Present State, and Future Prospects of the Law*. Edinburgh, 1835.

―――. "Joseph Story's First Writing on Equity." Edited by Gerald T. Dunne. *American Journal of Legal History* 14 (1970): 79.

―――. "Law, Legislation, and Codes." In *Encyclopedia Americana*, volume 7. Philadelphia, 1829–33.

―――. "Natural Law." Ibid., vol. 9.

Surrency, Erwin C. "The Judiciary Act of 1801." *American Journal of Legal History* 2 (1958): 53.

Van den Haag, Ernest. "Social Science Testimony in the Desegregation Cases—"A Reply to Professor Kenneth Clark." *Villanova Law Review* 6 (1960): 69.

Vinogradoff, Sir Paul. "Reason and Conscience in Sixteenth Century Jurisprudence." *Law Quarterly Review* 24 (1908): 373.

Wilson, S. D. "Courts of Chancery in the American Colonial Period." *American Law Review* 18 (1884): 226.

Index

Abraham, Henry J., ix–xi, xiv, 137 n.1
Adams, John Quincy, 71
aequitas, 19–20, 30
Aequitas sequitur legem, 5, 76
aequus, 19
Alexander v. *Hillman,* 101–5
Alexander v. *Holmes County Bd. of Education,* 116–17, 119
American Bar Association, 91
American Life Insurance v. *Stewart,* 151 n.32
Anti-Federalists: consolidation feared by, 43–44; on the dangers of equity, 1, 6–7, 43–44; judicial power feared by, 6–7, 43–44
Aristotle: influence of, on concept of equity, 15–18, 24, 32, 74–75; on juridical equity, xiii, 4–5, 15–18, 19, 75; on jurisprudence, 17–18; *Magna Moralia,* 15–16; *Nichomachean Ethics,* 15–17; *Politics,* 139 n.4; *Rhetoric,* 5, 15–17
Articles of Confederation, 60
Atlas Life Insurance v. *W. I. Southern, Inc.,* 108 n.32

Bacon, Sir Francis, 4–6, 25–29, 67, 74
Ballow, Henry, 32
Barber, Sotirios A., xiv, 130
Barker, Sir Ernest, 18
Bassett, Richard, 44
Battisti, Judge Frank, 3
Beal v. *Missouri Pacific Railroad Corp.,* 109 n.38
Beasley v. *Texas & Pacific Railway Co.,* 150 n.11
Bell, Judge Griffin, 114
Bell v. *City School of Gary, Indiana,* 112
Bennett v. *Butterworth,* 90
Bentham, Jeremy, 61, 85, 86
Berger, Raoul, 137 n.1
Bickel, Alexander M., 137 n.1
Black, Justice Hugo, 116, 129
Blackstone, Sir William, 4, 31–32, 42–43, 67, 76, 78, 84, 85

171

Index

Lincoln, Abraham, 135
Lincoln, Levi, 71
Livingston v. *Story,* 106 n.18
Louisiana v. *United States,* 115

McFaul v. *Ramsey,* 91
Machiavelli, Niccolò, 51–52
Maclay, William, 44–46
Madison, James: on the common law, 55–56, 60–61; correspondence of, with Peter S. DuPonceau, 64–65; in *The Federalist,* 130, 133; and the Jeffersonians, 56–60, 70–72; on judicial power, 10; in the Philadelphia Convention, 152 n.10, 153 n.37; and the Virginia Report, 60–61
Maine, Sir Henry, 19
Marbury v. *Madison,* 128
Marshall, Chief Justice John, 70, 125, 128
Mason, George, 43, 55–56
Massachusetts State Grange v. *Benton,* 98 n.5, 107 n.28, 108 n.33
Matthews v. *Rodgers,* 108 n.35
Meredith v. *Winter Haven,* 102
Miles v. *Caldwell,* 150 n.15
Mill, John Stuart, 123
Miller, Justice Samuel, 91, 108
Milliken v. *Bradley* (I), 4, 120
Milliken v. *Bradley* (II), 4, 10, 121, 127
Monarchy, English, 5, 24–32
Montesquieu, 125
Morris, Gouverneur, 152 n.10
Murphy, Justice Frank, 105

New Orleans City Park Improvement Association v. *Detiege,* 112 n.2

Osborn v. *Bank of the United States,* 102
Otis, Harrison Gray, 56–57
Otis, James, 141 n.6

Paine, Thomas, ix
Parker v. *Winnipiseogee,* 107–8 n.30
Pasadena City Board of Education v. *Spangler,* 120
Paterson, William, 44–46
Payne v. *Hook,* 150 n.16, 107 n.27
Pennsylvania v. *Wheeling,* 150 n.16
Pennsylvania v. *Williams,* 99 n.8, 108–9 n.37
Peters, Richard, 72
Petroleum Exploration Inc. v. *Public Service Commission of Kentucky,* 109 n.38
Philadelphia v. *Stimson,* 102–3

Index

Pinckney, Charles, 153 n.37
Pittman, Judge Virgil, 3
Pleadings: equitable, 81–82; legal, 81–82
Plessy v. *Ferguson*, 109, 131–32
Pollock, Sir Frederick, 24
Popular government: and legislative tyranny, 130–31; and popular tyranny, 130; and the problem of faction, 130–31
Porter v. *Warner*, 8, 105
Powell, Justice Lewis, 119–20
Praetor, role of, in developing principles of equity in Rome, 20–21
Process Act: of 1789, 7, 46; of 1792, 7, 46–47
Public interest, 8, 10, 102–3

quare clausum fregit, 38

Racial discrimination: and the "all deliberate speed" doctrine, 98–100, 111–21; and court-ordered busing, 117–19; and *de facto* segregation, 110, 119–20; and *de jure* segregation, 110, 116, 119–20, 131; and "freedom of choice" desegregation plans, 114–17; and inter-district busing, 120–21; and low-income housing, 120; and remedial-education programs, 120–21; and school desegregation, 97–99, 109–10, 111–21; and "separate but equal" doctrine, 98–99, 109, 131; and the transformation of prohibition of segregation into a demand for integration, 113–21
Railroad Commission of Texas v. *Pullman Co.*, 150 n.11, 109 n.38, 110 n.42
Randolph, Edmund: and the Jeffersonians, 57–59; "Notes on the Common Law," 57–59
Reason, 28–29, 34–35
Rees v. *Watertown*, 5 n.5, 102 n.10, 107
Rehnquist, Justice William, 120
Robinson v. *Campbell*, 106
Rossum, Ralph A., xiv, 143 n.4
Rules of Civil Procedure of 1938, 7–8, 51, 107; Advisory Committee on, 92; and Promulgation Act of 1934, 93
Rutgers v. *Waddington*, 37–40
Rutland, Robert A., xiv

St. Germain, Christopher, 4, 22–24, 25, 67
In re Sawyer, 103 n.14, 104
Schiro v. *Bynum*, 112 n.6
Schlatter, Richard, 143 n.3
Scottish: Enlightenment, 52–54; moral-sense philosophy, 52–54
Severus, Alexander, 31
Shelley v. *Kraemer*, 149 n.7

178

Index